★The★
Baseball
Hall of
SHAME

by

BRUCE NASH AND
ALLAN ZULLO

Bernie Ward, Curator

WALLABY

A WALLABY BOOK

PUBLISHED BY POCKET BOOKS NEW YORK

This book is dedicated to anyone who has ever booted an easy grounder, walked in the winning run, or struck out with the bases loaded.

ACKNOWLEDGMENT

We wish to thank all the thousands of fans, players, sports-writers and broadcasters who contributed nominations to The Baseball Hall of SHAME.

Another *Original* publication of WALLABY BOOKS

A Wallaby Book published by
POCKET BOOKS, a division of Simon & Schuster, Inc.
1230 Avenue of the Americas, New York, N.Y. 10020

ISBN: 0-671-52485-2

First Wallaby Books printing April, 1985

10 9 8 7 6 5 4 3 2 1

WALLABY and colophon are registered trademarks
of Simon & Schuster, Inc.

Designed by Joe Marc Freedman

Printed in the U.S.A.

Contents

Leading Off

It's time to give discredit where discredit is due.

For over a century, baseball has immortalized the home run slugger, the clean-cut All-American, the golden glover, the big-hearted lug, the unstoppable dynasty. But the truth is winners and nice guys and heroes are boring.

Who really makes the grand old game so entertaining, rousing, and exciting? The losers, the cheaters, the flakes, the buffoons, the boneheads, the inept, the outrageous, the obnoxious. They have given real demeaning to the word baseball. They have brought color to the game—a black eye. They are the true foul balls whose contributions have withstood the detest of time.

Yet where is their niche in the Hall of Fame? Nowhere. To correct this travesty of sports injustice, we founded The Baseball Hall of SHAME. Cooperstown can have baseball's shining stars. The Hall of SHAME wants baseball's shiners.

The history of our national pastime boasts a rich heritage of shameful moments both on and off the field by teams, players, managers, coaches, owners, general managers, umpires, groundskeepers, and even the fans themselves.

To help us choose the most deserving candidates for Baseball Hall of SHAME dishonors, we made a nationwide appeal in the spring of 1984 to fans, sportswriters, broadcasters, and players for nominations. We spread the word on radio from coast to coast and throughout Canada. We went on TV and were interviewed in scores of newspapers and magazines. We visited spring training camps where we received nominations in the bleachers, clubhouses, dugouts, and press boxes. Then we spent weeks sifting through record books, archival material, and faded newspaper accounts. We considered all shameful moments and tossed out those which involved drugs or murder since there's nothing funny about either.

However, most everything else shameful had a chance of being selected for dishonors.

Not everyone who blundered on or off the field belongs in The Baseball Hall of SHAME. In our judgment, only a small select number of the thousands of boners and disgraces that have tainted the game met our unique standards for inclusion in the Hall's first induction.

However, we don't intend to stop here. Periodically, we will be considering prospective Hall of Shamers from the past and present for enshrinement. If you feel some baseball personality or moment is deserving of such dishonors, we want to know about it. Please send us your nominations of hilarious happenings and ignoble incidents. To learn how to submit your picks, turn to page 187.

We want The Baseball Hall of SHAME to be the fans' shrine. We're not out to make fun of baseball. Instead, we want to have fun with the game we all love. This book is more than just the official record of charter membership in The Baseball Hall of SHAME. It's also a way for fans across the country to pay a light-hearted tribute to the national pastime. We have found that superstars and bozos have one thing in common—they all screw up. (It's just that some screw up more than others.)

As you read through this book, we hope you come to the same conclusion we did. We can all identify with—and laugh about—each inductee's shameful moment because each one of us has at one time or another pulled a "rock."

Welcome to the Bigs!

The Most Inauspicious Major League Debuts

Aspiring major leaguers dream about what that glorious first day in the bigs will be like. They see themselves hammering the winning home run with two out in the bottom of the ninth or leaping high against the fence to make a game-saving catch. That's the fantasy. The reality is that in their diamond debuts they often stumble over their feet, fall flat on their faces or otherwise disgrace themselves so badly they carry a stigma with them the rest of their careers—which can be a whole lot shorter than they planned. For "The Most Inauspicious Major League Debuts," The Baseball Hall of SHAME inducts the following:

Harry Heitman
PITCHER · BROOKLYN, N.L. · JULY 27, 1918

Harry Heitman holds a dishonor no other can claim. Hapless Harry is the first inductee into The Baseball Hall of SHAME—and he deserves it.

    Against St. Louis in his very first game, Heitman had barely warmed up when the Cardinals—and everlasting shame—came crashing down on his head like a ton of bats. He faced five batters and managed to get only one out. The other four hitters ripped him for two singles and two triples before he was yanked.

Heitman staggered off the mound with a whopping ERA of 108.00. Owning a stat like that, Heitman did the only thing he could. He tossed his glove away and enlisted in the Navy that very afternoon. He never pitched in the majors again.

Bruno Haas

PITCHER · PHILADELPHIA, A.L. · JUNE 23, 1915

Fresh out of Worcester Academy where baseball was still played as a gentleman's game, Bruno Haas learned quickly that the baseball field of honor can be pure hell.

Starting against the Yankees in his debut, Haas strode to the mound in his new Philadelphia uniform. But any similarity between him and a major league pitcher ended there. Haas gave up 15 runs and 11 hits—which wasn't so bad considering he couldn't get the ball over the plate.

Like a generous circus owner, Haas gave free passes to everyone in pinstripes. By the end of the day he had walked 16 batters, a mark unequalled for a nine inning game. In case anybody doubted his wildness, he also uncorked three wild pitches.

At the end of the year, Haas vanished from the majors. Some said he just "walked" away.

George Brace Photo

Billy Herman

SECOND BASEMAN · CHICAGO, N.L. · AUG. 29, 1931

Billy Herman can't remember a whole lot about his big league debut. It's just as well.

Thrilled at getting a chance to break into the starting lineup, Billy was determined to prove he belonged. Batting against Cincinnati Reds hurler Si Johnson, Billy dug into the batter's box.

Johnson threw and Billy took a tremendous swing. The ball hit the ground in back of the plate and, with wicked reverse English, bounced straight back, smacking Billy right on the head.

So a sterling career that spanned two decades and ended with a .304 lifetime batting average started out in the most ignominious way possible. Billy Herman was carried off the field on a stretcher—knocked out cold by his own foul ball!

The New York Mets

APRIL 11, 1962

The debut of the new franchise from New York set the tone for a season in which the Mets emerged as America's favorite four-letter word.

Trouble began on the eve of opening day in St. Louis when 16 Mets got stuck in the Chase Hotel elevator for 20 minutes. It was a definite omen.

The next day, in their very first game, the Mets' fortunes plunged straight into the basement in an 11–4 loss. But what made this debut so pitiful was their first-inning performance.

With Cardinal runner Bill White on third, New York pitcher Roger Craig looked in for the sign and checked the runner. Then Craig went into his stretch . . . and dropped the ball. Dumbfounded, Craig watched the umpire wave White home.

The New York Mets had given up the first run in the history of the franchise on a balk!

The Bottom of the Barrel

The Worst Teams of All Time

Some teams belong at the top of the standings. Others belong in a Marx Brothers movie. Their pitchers have trouble finding the mound let alone home plate. Their hitters get no-hit in batting practice. And their fielders act like they're auditioning for a vaudeville routine. Right from opening day, these teams tumble directly into the cellar—and stay there. For "The Worst Teams of All Time," The Baseball Hall of SHAME inducts the following:

The Cleveland Spiders

1899

The Cleveland Spiders of 1899 were certifiably the worst team in baseball history.

.Wallowing in the basement of the 12-team National League, these laughable losers piled up an amazing 134 losses against only 20 wins for the all-time lowest winning percentage of .130. They finished 84 games out of first, making the rest of history's lousiest teams seem like pennant contenders.

. The Spiders were last in runs, doubles, triples, homers, batting average, slugging percentage, and stolen bases. They were outscored by a two-to-one margin, 1,252 runs to 529.

Appropriately enough, the Spiders lost the first game of the season 10–1 to start their losing habit. Six different times they recorded losing streaks of eleven or more games. Once in Brooklyn, they found themselves in an unfamiliar situation—leading 10–1 after six innings. Refusing to bow to victory, they managed to pull out the defeat by an 11–10 score.

With losses piling up left and right, manager Lave Cross quit in disgust before the end of the first month.

Blame the team's abysmal record on the owners, brothers Frank and Matthew Robison, who knew little about baseball. Rather than hire more talent before the season started, they bought a second team, the St. Louis Browns, and then set about dissecting the Spiders.

To guarantee failure of the Spiders, the Brothers Robison shipped their best players, including Cy Young, to the Browns. Young won 26 games for St. Louis that season—six more than his former team won all year.

With the way the Cleveland hurlers pitched and their opponents hit, it's a wonder the Spider fielders weren't maimed by all the line drives. The two "aces" on the staff, Charlie Knepper and Jim Hughey, each won a paltry four games and together were responsible for 52 losses.

The Spiders were so bad that even their own loved ones wouldn't come out to watch them. As a result, they played only 41 games of the 154-game schedule in Cleveland. They would have played more games on the road except the fed-up fans in other cities made the Spiders go home.

Fittingly, the Spiders ended the season by dropping 40 of their last 41 games. In their final game, they recruited a hotel cigar counter clerk to pitch for them against the Cincinnati Reds. In true Spider tradition, he lost 19–3.

The following year, the league voted to reduce the number of teams, and to no one's surprise, the Spiders were stomped out of existence.

The Philadelphia Athletics
1916

Two years after winning the pennant, manager Connie Mack conducted one of his periodic house cleanings. He swept out his talented stars to make way for cheaper rookies, stumblebums, and other assorted cast offs willing to play for slave wages.

He got what he paid for—a deplorable team that ended the 1916 season with a sickening 36–117 record and a .235 winning percentage, the worst in modern history. They finished 54½ games out of first, so far back that even on a clear day they couldn't see the seventh-place Senators who were 40 games ahead of them.

More than anything else, it was the terrible pitching that turned the once-proud A's into F's. One of the stars that Mack kept was righthander Bullet Joe Bush, much to the lasting embarrassment of Bullet Joe. Forced to take his regular turn on the mound, he lost 22 games, barely getting nosed out by teammate Elmer Myers' 23 defeats for most losses in the league. Hurler Jack Nabors won the first game he pitched that season and then rested on his laurel. Nabors lost his next 19 decisions, earning him a tie in the record book for the most consecutive games lost in a season.

After his awful record-breaking season, Nabors dropped out of sight. Unfortunately, Mack and the rest of the A's didn't. The next year, the A's finished last again, 44½ games back.

The Philadelphia Phillies

1961

It was a rainy night in Philadelphia, but a deliriously happy mob of baseball fans filled the International Airport, complete with victory banners and brass bands to welcome home the Phils. Manager Gene Mauch was hoisted onto the fans' shoulders and carried triumphantly through the terminal. Almost overcome with emotion, Mauch told the roaring crowd that it was "hard to believe how these kids kept battling through all those games. It's something to make these players proud."

A pennant winner come home? A World Series champ? No-o-o-o!

The Phillies had finally won a game after four straight winless weeks. When the victory drought ended, they had established a modern era record by losing 23 games in a row.

The Phillies weren't just a so-so team on a bad luck roll. They stunk up the league all year long, winning only 47 games and losing 107.

They trudged their way into immortality by consistently blowing close games they should have won. Take the game that tied the record of 20 consecutive losses. The Phillies lost a two-run lead in the eighth inning against the Braves and were forced into extra frames. The Phils wriggled out of a bases-loaded, tenth inning jam with a nifty double play. In the next inning they met the challenge head on and did what they usually did best—they gave the game away on two walks and an error.

The Phillies set a new record for futility the next day when the Braves' Lew Burdette buzz-sawed them on a three-hitter. The frustration continued in loss number 22. The Phillies whacked 12 hits but left men on base in every inning—and wasted a no-out, bases-loaded opportunity in the ninth— before going down to a 4–3 defeat.

But all bad things must come to an end. After losing the first game of a double-header, the Phils finally tasted victory, beating the Braves 7–4 behind pitcher John Buzhardt on August 20. Nobody was happier than

Buzhardt over his fourth win of the season. He happened to be the last Phillies pitcher to win a game since the losing streak started on July 28.

A footnote to the great Philly Flop: Pitching ace Robin Roberts started the 1961 season with 233 career wins. He finished the year with 234 wins.

The New York Mets

1962

The Mets were the most hilarious bunch of has-beens and never-would-be's ever to step onto a diamond. They had a lineup that even Rodney Dangerfield couldn't respect.

With all the wrong stuff, they stumbled to an inglorious 40–120 season which left manager Casey Stengel to marvel: "They've shown me ways to lose I never knew existed."

It took them 10 games before they finally figured out how to win. But within a few weeks they went on a 17-game losing streak that assured their place in infamy.

The Mets had two problems. Either they were too young or too old. The gaggle of over-the-hillers included such players as Richie Ashburn, Gus Bell, Wilmer "Vinegar Bend" Mizell, Gil Hodges, and 40-year-old Gene Woodling, who later said that his favorite memory of the 1962 season was going home when it was all over.

Early in the season, veteran Don Zimmer, Met third baseman, went 0 for 34 at the plate. When he finally broke out of his slump with a single, the Mets quickly traded him to the Reds. They wanted to deal Zimmer while he was hot. In exchange for Zimmer, the Mets received rookie Cliff Cook, a promising power hitter and third sacker. There was only one problem. Cook had a slipped disk in his back and couldn't bend over.

That year the Mets went through nine catchers. Each, it seemed, had his own specialty. Choo Choo Coleman could catch but he couldn't hit or throw. Hobie Landrith could hit but he couldn't catch or throw. Harry Chiti couldn't do any of the above. New York had obtained him from Cleveland for a player to be named later. When the Mets discovered that Chiti was no major league catcher—even by Met standards—they unloaded him. And since they owed Cleveland a player, they sent Chiti. Only the Mets could have pulled off a deal like this—trading Chiti for himself.

So many players kept coming and going that the Met clubhouse looked more like Grand Central Station. Another early-season trade brought the team a balding, veteran first baseman whose good years—if you could call them good—were behind him. His name was Marvelous Marv Throneberry.

He could make the worst out of any situation. It wasn't that he was such a bad first baseman. It was just that he had trouble handling throws, judging popups and fielding grounders. But the fans loved him anyway and they bestowed upon him the title of Mr. Met. He represented everything that was wrong with the team. Speaking to the fans between games of a double-header, he said, "I'd tell you a few jokes, but there are already plenty of comedians around here."

Leading the Mets to the first tenth place finish in modern National League history, the pitching staff coughed up 192 homers, 1,577 hits and 801 earned runs. Pitcher Jay Hook contributed 137 of those tallies all by himself. A graduate engineer, Hook had a much easier time explaining the curve ball than throwing one.

On the final game of the season, the Mets lost to the Cubs 5–1 in a contest low-lighted by their becoming victims of an eighth-inning triple play.

After the game, the Ol' Professor, who had enjoyed many a happy day as the Yankee skipper, lamented, "I won with this club what I used to lose."

Nevertheless, this band of cast offs and cutups endeared themselves to New Yorkers. One psychologist told *The New York Times* that rooting for the Mets was "a kind of masochism." If that's true, imagine how it felt *playing* for the Mets.

Holey Mitts!

The Most Inept Fielding Performances

You can tell who they are by their first initial, E. They are the fabulous fumblers who somehow make it to the bigs with holes in their gloves. These players catch hell from fans more often than balls—which are handled as if they're grenades. These guys boot so many balls they belong on a soccer field, not a baseball diamond. For "The Most Inept Fielding Performances," The Baseball Hall of SHAME inducts the following:

Smead Jolley
OUTFIELDER · CHICAGO-BOSTON, A.L. · 1930–33

Smead Jolley was one of the world's worst outfielders. Even Jolley agreed.

He sealed his reputation by committing three errors on a single play. He was stationed in right field in a game against the Athletics in Philadelphia. Bing Miller smashed a single and, to the White Sox's dismay, it headed right for Jolley.

As expected, the ball rolled through his legs for error number one. Jolley whirled around to play the carom off the wall. To no one's surprise, the ball scooted back through his legs for error number two. Jolley could have stopped while he was ahead, but perhaps sensing immortality, he seized the moment to vault himself into the twilight zone of fielding. He picked up the ball and heaved it over the third baseman's head for error number three. Meanwhile, Bing Miller circled the bases.

Shockingly, Jolley's incredible feat never made it into the record books. The official scorer, refusing to believe that any major leaguer could commit such a fielding atrocity, charged Jolley with only two errors, thus robbing him of an officially recognized record as the worst single fielding play in baseball history.

Nevertheless, Jolley went on to distinguish himself when he was traded to the Boston Red Sox where he had trouble with Fenway Park. Some parks in those days had embankments against the outfield fences before warning tracks were installed. At that time, Fenway had a ten-foot incline in left field. To Jolley it was as awesome as Mount Everest. In frustration, the Red Sox coaches spent mornings hitting fungoes to left while Jolley practiced running up the hill to make the catch.

The next time Jolley started in left, he had a chance to show how he could handle the incline. In a game against the Washington Senators, a long fly ball was hit to left. Jolley took off, ran easily up the incline, turned around to make the catch and saw that he had overrun the ball. Jolley started back down the incline but tripped and sprawled flat on his face. The ball bounced near him and by the time Jolley staggered to his feet, the batter was standing on third.

At the end of the inning, Jolley returned to the dugout, cussing at his coaches. "Fine bunch, you guys," he complained. "For ten days you teach me how to go up the hill, but none of you has the brains to teach me how to come down!"

George Brace Photo

AP/Wide World Photo

Dick Stuart

FIRST BASEMAN · PHILADELPHIA-PITTSBURGH-NEW YORK-
LOS ANGELES, N.L. · CALIFORNIA-BOSTON, A.L. · 1958—69

Dick Stuart collected almost as many nicknames during his career as he did errors—and those came by the bushel. Come to think of it, a bushel basket was what he needed at first base instead of the sieve he used for a glove.

Stuart is remembered as "Dr. Strangeglove," "Stonefingers," and "Clank" for the sound of the ball bouncing off his hands. He not only deserved the monikers, he loved them. In a touch of class that only a true Hall of Shamer could appreciate, Stuart ordered a specially made vanity license plate for his car that proclaimed to the world, "E-3."

Stuart knew he was in trouble if he attempted to get into the record books by hitting more homers or running up a higher average than everyone else. He didn't have that much talent. Instead, he decided to specialize in one area—errors.

For seven straight years, from 1958 through 1964, Stuart led the majors or tied for the lead in the number of errors for a season by a first baseman— a low mark yet to be challenged.

For five of those years he turned first base in Pittsburgh into such a mess that the mayor wanted it declared a disaster area.

Stuart basked in his notoriety. "Errors are part of my image," he used to brag. "One night in Pittsburgh, thirty thousand fans gave me a standing ovation when I caught a hot dog wrapper on the fly."

Andy Pafko

OUTFIELDER · CHICAGO, N.L. · APRIL 30, 1949

Andy Pafko was known for his diving lunges for Texas Leaguers and sinking line drives. Sometimes he caught them and came up smelling like a rose. Other times he missed them and came up smelling. Then there was the time when he lost the catch, his head, and the game.

In front of a near-capacity crowd at Wrigley Field, the Cubs held a 3–2 lead over the Cardinals with two out and a man on first in the top of the ninth inning. St. Louis batter Rocky Nelson then hit a low liner to center field. Pafko raced in on a dead run and appeared to snag the ball for the final out as he made a diving somersault. He held up the ball to show the cheering crowd. But his joy turned to shock when second base umpire Al Barlick signaled no catch.

Furious, Pafko raced over to Barlick and shouted loudly that he had made the catch. Barlick shook his head. Pafko was so intent on arguing that he failed to realize the ball he held in his glove was still in play.

As Pafko ranted and raved, the runner on first scored the tying run. Meanwhile, Rocky Nelson didn't even slow down. He passed the Pafko-Barlick debate at second, made the turn at third and headed for home. By now the other Cubs were screaming at Pafko to throw the ball. Finally, the message sank in and Pafko fired the ball in desperation to the plate. But the ball popped out of the catcher's mitt and Nelson slid across with the winning run.

Thanks to Pafko's lapse, his team lost—on an inside-the-glove home run.

Bill Melton

THIRD BASEMAN · CHICAGO-CALIFORNIA-CLEVELAND, A.L.
1968–77

Bill Melton was one of those "good-hit, no-field" plumbers at third base who could drive in three runs in a game with his bat but give up four runs with his fielding.

In 1970, when Melton played for the White Sox, he endured one of the most embarrassing first months of any major leaguer. He committed a whopping 10 errors in the Sox's first 24 games. That was bad enough.

Even worse was the broken nose he suffered in a May 7 game in

Baltimore. First, he fumbled a routine grounder in the third inning for his eleventh error of the season. Then three innings later came the final ignobility.

Melton camped under a high foul popup, ready to make a routine catch—routine, that is, for most fielders. In typical Melton fashion, the ball struck the heel of his glove and then smashed into his nose. He went down like a poled ox, knocked unconscious for a couple of minutes.

The official scorer had no choice but to add insult to injury: "It's got to be another error. There's no other way you can call it."

As Melton regained consciousness and was placed in the ambulance, he muttered, "The way things are going this had to happen. I'm not surprised." Neither were his teammates.

Joe DiMaggio

OUTFIELDER · NEW YORK, A.L. · JULY 30, 1951

In all his thirteen years in baseball, Joe DiMaggio never suffered a mental lapse on the field—except once.

Through 1,684 regular season games, 45 World Series contests and 10 All-Star games, the Yankee Clipper had never been known to throw to the wrong base, try for an extra base without a good chance of reaching safely, or be guilty of daydreaming out in the field. But DiMaggio, the thinking man's ball player whom teammates and fans always counted on for his rock-solid dependability, committed an embarrassing blunder in his 1,685th game.

It came at a most inopportune time. In the top of the eighth inning in a game against Detroit, Tigers star George Kell was on second base with one out and his team ahead 3–2.

The next batter, Steve Souchock, flied to deep center where DiMaggio made the catch. Unbelievably, Joe leisurely started to trot in with the ball, thinking erroneously that there were three outs. But Kell knew differently. He tagged up at second and headed toward third where coach Dick Bartell waved him around. By the time DiMaggio woke up from his mental fog, Kell was racing for home. DiMaggio's blunder allowed Kell—who could run only slightly faster than Bess Truman—to score from second base on an outfield fly.

The 39,684 fans gasped in disbelief. Joe DiMaggio, the closest thing to a perfect player, had pulled a boner—one that put the home team down by two runs, 4–2, with only two innings left to play.

Joltin' Joe was so ashamed that there was only one way to atone for his mistake. In the bottom of the ninth inning, after the Yankees had tied the score, he drove in the winning run.

Swap Slop

The Dumbest Trades Ever Made

General managers claim they make trades to better the team. But it's often the other team they make better. Baseball is blighted with execs who couldn't recognize talent at the All-Star Game. With their skills at dealing, these GMs would trade their new Cadillac for a rusty Volkswagen and an Edsel to be named later. For "The Dumbest Trades Ever Made," The Baseball Hall of SHAME inducts the following:

Lou Brock for Ernie Broglio

EARLY IN THE 1964 SEASON

The Chicago Cubs front office was fleeced in broad daylight by the St. Louis Cardinals. And, boy, did it hurt. Only the Great Fire did more damage to the Windy City.

Brock showed tremendous potential as a fleet-footed outfielder. But 52 games into the 1964 season, the Cubs gave up on him and his .251 batting average. They sent Brock packing to St. Louis in exchange for pitcher Ernie Broglio as part of a six-player deal.

Once he donned a Cardinal uniform, Brock hit .348 and stole 33 bases to lead his team to the first of three pennants and two world championships during the 1960s. Brock made the world forget the likes of Ty Cobb and Maury Wills when he swiped a record 118 bases in 1974 and ended his career with 3,023 hits.

Broglio turned out to be a sore-armed pitcher who posted a dismal 4–

7 record in his first year with the Cubs. Before he was booed out of Chicago two years later, he won only three more games.

Ever since, he has had to bear the burden of the Cubs' stupidity. This may explain why, when he retired, he built a bonfire on his front lawn and tossed in his equipment—uniform, shoes, gloves, cap, socks, and jock strap.

George Foster for Frank Duffy and Vern Geishert

EARLY IN THE 1971 SEASON

After this lopsided trade with Cincinnati, San Francisco fans were convinced the Giants front office consisted of losers from "Let's Make A Deal."

Foster was a promising young outfielder when the Giants traded him away. As a Red, Foster became one of the most feared sluggers in baseball. He led the league twice in homers and three times in RBIs and hit over .300 four times. In 1977 he won the MVP award after swatting 52 homers and driving in 149 runs.

Duffy spent his first year with the Giants trying to play shortstop and pretending he was a hitter with a sickening .179 average before he was shipped to Cleveland.

The other player in the deal, Vern Geishert, wasn't even worth loose change. Geishert, who had won only one game in the bigs prior to the trade, didn't even make the team.

Frank Robinson for Milt Pappas

END OF THE 1965 SEASON

Reds General Manager Bill DeWitt decided that at age thirty Frank Robinson was getting too old to be of much use anymore. Because of that decision, Cincinnati fans felt DeWitt wasn't of much use anymore.

DeWitt "persuaded" the Orioles to take Robinson in exchange for pitcher Milt Pappas. In two seasons with the Reds, Pappas won 30 and lost 29. Not much excitement there.

Meanwhile, "old man" Robinson won the Triple Crown with a .316 batting average, 49 homers and 122 RBIs in his first year with the Orioles, helping bring a pennant to Baltimore. In the World Series, he smashed two homers in the Orioles' four-game rout of the Dodgers. That same year, Robinson was voted the league's MVP, the first and only player to win the honor in both leagues. He went on to help power the Orioles to three more pennants and another world championship.

Christy Mathewson for Amos Rusie

BEFORE THE 1900 SEASON

The Cincinnati front office was cheering. They had just obtained Giants star hurler Amos Rusie. All they had to give up was this kid named Christy Mathewson, who was fresh out of college. It didn't take long for those Cincy cheers to turn to tears.

Mathewson matured into one of the game's all-time great pitchers, racking up an incredible 373 career victories, all but one with the Giants.

To the dismay of the Reds, Rusie appeared in only three games after the trade and didn't win a single one. He ended up later in life back at the Polo Grounds. As an attendant.

Norm Cash for Steve Demeter

END OF THE 1959 SEASON

Steve Demeter was a third baseman who played 11 games for Detroit in 1959 and hit a paltry .111. For some insane reason, Cleveland wanted him anyway. The Indians traded Norm Cash, whom they had just acquired from the White Sox, for Demeter.

After the swap, Demeter saw action in just four games, had a perfect batting average of .000 and, to the relief of the red-faced Indians, disappeared.

Cash did somewhat better. Two years after the trade, he won the batting title with a .361 average, slammed 41 homers and drove in 132 runs. Cash closed out his 17-year career with 377 home runs and 1,103 RBIs.

Billy Pierce for Aaron Robinson

END OF THE 1948 SEASON

Pierce was 3–0 as a twenty-one-year-old pitcher for the Tigers when they decided to go with experience. They wanted 33-year-old White Sox catcher Aaron Robinson. Chicago got Pierce. Detroit got the shaft.

During his 13-year career with the White Sox, Pierce was a 20-game winner twice and at various times led the league in games won, strikeouts, and ERA. Pierce finished with 211 regular season wins and a World Series victory.

Robinson lasted two more lackluster years with Detroit. In 1951, he appeared in only 36 games for the Tigers who then palmed him off to Boston where he played in 26 more games and then retired.

Charles "Red" Ruffing for Cedric Durst

BEGINNING OF THE 1930 SEASON

Boston Red Sox owner Harry Frazee was a slow learner. The same guy who peddled Babe Ruth to the Yankees for a pittance blew another deal.

Durst was a so-so utility outfielder whom the Yankees were more than happy to send to Boston. It proved to be his last year in the majors.

The righthanded Ruffing pitched for another 16 years. In fact, he won more than twice as many games for the Yankees (231) than Durst even played for the Red Sox (102). Ruffing was the first pitcher to win seven World Series games.

Long after Frazee left the front office, Boston was still being painfully reminded of his dumb trade. Four different times while Ruffing was in New York, the Yankees and Red Sox finished one-two in the pennant race. In three of those years, Ruffing's victories provided the winning edge for the Yankees.

Marilyn Peterson for Susanne Kekich

MIDDLE OF THE 1972 SEASON

In what they called the "most unique trade in baseball," New York Yankees pitchers Fritz Peterson and Mike Kekich stunned the civilized baseball establishment by swapping wives, children, and even the family dogs.

AP/Wide World Photo

Peterson's wife Marilyn moved in with Mike while Susanne Kekich took up house with Fritz. Each couple had two children so it was decided that the older child of each marriage would stay with his father while the younger one lived with his mother.

The trade seemed to be working so well that they contemplated not only a double divorce but a double wedding. However, a few months later, the arrangement engineered by the switch pitchers collapsed. Marilyn went home to mother. Kekich was traded—the conventional way—and life between Fritz and Susanne soured.

Mumbled Yankee General Manager Lee MacPhail: "We may have to call off Family Day."

Nellie Fox for Joe Tipton

END OF THE 1949 SEASON

Looking for a catcher, the Philadelphia A's found their man—the White Sox's Joe Tipton. Never mind that he was an undistinguished hitter and considered a troublemaker.

The A's offered the White Sox a stubby, twenty-three-year-old infielder named Nellie Fox. Little Fox became one of baseball's best second sackers, known for his accurate bat and his superb fielding. Fox led the league four times in hits, went 12 years with the fewest strikeouts and was named the league's MVP in 1959.

Joe Tipton, however, doesn't even rate a question in a trivia game. Until he quit in 1954, Tipton spent most of his time in the bullpen warming up relief pitchers.

Nolan Ryan for Jim Fregosi

END OF THE 1971 SEASON

This deal would have made a snake oil salesman grin.

For years, the Mets had been looking for a regular third baseman. So what did they do? They traded for an overweight shortstop, one they tried to convert into a third baseman. In exchange for Fregosi, the California Angels received young, fireballing strikeout-artist Nolan Ryan.

Fregosi, then the forty-sixth man to play third base for the Mets, was, like all the others before him, a bust. The first ball hit to him in a spring training game went between his legs. The next day he broke his finger. Dealt away two and a half years later, he hit only .233 for the Mets.

Meanwhile, Ryan established himself as one of baseball's great pitchers, twirling 5 no-hitters and setting a new record by whiffing 383 batters in a single season.

Every Trick in the Book

The Sneakiest Cheating Perpetrated by Players

To be a major leaguer, you first need to learn the basic fundamentals of the game such as laying down a bunt, running the bases, making the pivot on a double play. But to gain that extra edge which could mean the difference between winning and losing, players need to learn the finer points—how to doctor a bat, cut up a baseball, and other nifty illegal tricks of the trade. For "The Sneakiest Cheating Perpetrated by Players," The Baseball Hall of SHAME inducts the following:

Norm Cash

FIRST BASEMAN-OUTFIELDER · CHICAGO-DETROIT, A.L.
1958–74

One of baseball's unwritten rules is "Do anything you can get away with." Stormin' Norman followed that rule to the letter. He once boasted, "I owe my success to expansion pitching, a short right field fence, and my hollow bats." Cash even went a step beyond just bragging about his cheating. He demonstrated in sports magazines for all the kids in America how to doctor a bat.

It took him only about an hour to turn his bat into an unlawful piece of lumber. Cash bored a hole about eight inches deep and a half inch wide into the fat end of the bat. He left most of the hole empty, but plugged the top couple of inches with cork sawdust and glue so it looked like a regulation bat. With the Cash touch, the mass of a 36-ounce bat took on the whiplash quickness of a 34-ouncer. And a bat with the lively corked center could add 50 feet to the distance the ball traveled.

In 1961 Cash hit 41 homers, collected 132 RBIs and won the batting title with a .361 average—all done, he admitted, with an illegal bat.

That's shameful enough. Even worse, however, is that in 1962 he again used the illicit timber but only hit a paltry .243!

Whitey Ford

PITCHER · NEW YORK, A.L. · 1950, 1953–67

In the last half of his remarkable career, Whitey Ford relied on his experience—at cheating. He was one of the best at throwing spitters, mud balls, and cut balls.

In fact, he used some chicanery during the fourth game of the 1963 World Series to make the ball do strange and unnatural things on the way to the plate. "I threw mostly mud balls and cut balls the whole game," Ford confessed later. "I had pretty good luck, too, because the Dodgers got only two hits off me." Frank Howard got both hits, a homer and run-scoring single, as Ford and the Yankees lost 2–1. "I guess I didn't cut the ball enough," Ford said ruefully.

Other teams tried to catch Ford in the act but he was always too clever. Whenever he felt he was being eyeballed too closely, he let his battery mate Elston Howard cut the ball on a little metal rivet on Howard's shinguard before tossing the ball back to Ford.

The *pièce de résistance* in Ford's bag of dirty tricks was *the ring*. He had this devilish little device made for him late in his career when his arm started to go. It was a stainless steel ring with a piece of rasp (a file with cutting points) cleverly welded on.

"I'd wear the ring on my right hand and since I'm lefthanded, that was my glove hand," Ford explained years later. "So during games, I'd just stand behind the mound like any other pitcher rubbing up a new ball and I'd take the glove off and rub up the ball. That rasp would do some job on it too. Whenever I needed a ground ball, I'd cut it good. It was as though I had my own tool bench out there with me."

It was such second nature for him to tinker with the ball that he couldn't shake the habit even after he retired. He once stooped so low that he cut a ball while pitching in an Old Timers game.

Rick Honeycutt

PITCHER · SEATTLE, A.L. · SEPT. 30, 1980

Rick Honeycutt was an embarrassment to cheaters everywhere. He got caught.

During the third inning of a game against the Kansas City Royals in Seattle's Kingdome, the Royals grew suspicious of the special effects of Honeycutt's pitches. The players asked plate umpire Bill Kunkel to check the ball and Honeycutt's glove hand. On close examination, the ump discovered a thumb tack taped to the pitcher's index finger. He also found a piece of sandpaper attached to the tape.

Kunkel thumbed the pitcher out of the game for his bumbling effort at cheating. As Honeycutt went slinking off the field, he felt so mortified that he forgot all about the tack and wiped his hand across his brow— leaving a bright red scratch across his forehead.

"I haven't been in trouble like that since the last time I was sent to the principal's office," admitted Honeycutt, who was fined $250 and suspended for ten days. "What an ordeal. Crime never pays."

Maury Wills

MANAGER · SEATTLE, A.L. · APRIL 25, 1981

Here's a friendly little tip from the Maury Wills handbook on "How to Beat a Curve Ball": When nobody is around, you order your chief groundskeeper to lengthen the batter's box toward the mound. That way, when a curveball specialist, say somebody like Rick Langford from the Oakland A's, comes to town, your hitters can move up an extra foot and swing at the curve before it breaks.

Wills actually tried to pull off this naughty deed. He might have succeeded except moments before the game, the Oakland manager spotted something fishy and asked umpire Bill Kunkel to check the dimensions of the box. Kunkel found it had been tampered with. The box was seven feet long instead of the regulation six and the extra foot was in the direction of the mound. For this bit of gardening, Wills was handed a two-game suspension and an undisclosed fine.

Wills' big mistake was trying to con a con man. The Oakland manager with the eagle eye for this sort of trickery was none other than Billy Martin.

Dave Danforth

PITCHER · PHILADELPHIA-CHICAGO-ST. LOUIS, A.L. · 1911–25

Dave Danforth is the patron saint of pitching-mound skulduggery.

In 1915, he invented the "shine" ball in Louisville where oil was used to settle the infield dust. He discovered that when he rubbed the oil and dirt off his pants leg, the unsoiled ball became smooth and did some fancy hopping.

Danforth was kicked out of a game in 1923 when one of his doctored balls "sailed" on him and nearly knocked off the head of A's outfielder Wid Matthews. The incident caused such an uproar over Danforth's unorthodox pitches that Commissioner Kenesaw Mountain Landis and American League President Ban Johnson both made trips to St. Louis just to watch how Danforth pitched against the Yankees. Umpire Billy Evans was ordered to keep feeding Danforth new balls. Before the game ended, he had used fifty-eight balls, a couple of dozen more than average. No one caught him in the act.

However, some opposing players insisted that Danforth didn't need any special equipment to fix the ball. They claimed that he was so strong he could squeeze the ball enough to stretch the cover and raise a lump. And that's why his ball could dance like a Mexican jumping bean.

Hitless Wonders

The Most Inept Batting Performances

Every team is saddled with terrible hitters, guys who buy a round of drinks if they go 1-for-5. They hit for averages that aren't even good for bowling. With that kind of dreadful batsmanship, these players couldn't hit the floor if they fell out of bed. They would strike out trying to hit the ball off a T-ball stand. For "The Most Inept Batting Performances," The Baseball Hall of SHAME inducts the following:

Bob Buhl

PITCHER · MILWAUKEE-CHICAGO-PITTSBURGH, N.L. · 1953–67

Bob Buhl is the idol of hitless wonders everywhere, a living reminder of incompetence with the bat. He went 0 for 1962. Seventy times he strode to the plate that year and 70 times he failed to get so much as a scratch single.

He was such an awful batter that he received standing ovations for hitting foul tips. He survived in the majors for 14 years with a career batting average of a microscopic .089. Buhl did swat some extra base hits, however. Once in 1956 and another time in 1958.

Batterless Buhl is best remembered for his hitless streak that started with the Braves in 1961 and ended with the Cubs in 1963. During that time, Buhl went through 42 games and 88 at bats without a hit to set a major league record.

He could have kept the streak going if Mother Nature hadn't intervened. On May 8, 1963, at Wrigley Field, Buhl hit a popup that a gust of wind blew out of the reach of the third baseman and shortstop who tripped over each other going after the ball. It fell for a single.

"They wanted to stop the game and give me the ball," Buhl said. With the eye of a true loser, Buhl analyzed his career at the plate. "The hits I had were accidental, really. I tried everything. I was a righthander but I tried batting lefthanded for a while. That didn't work. The only thing I didn't try was an ironing board.

"I hope my record stands. I think it should. I don't think anyone would want to break it."

Mario Mendoza

INFIELDER · PITTSBURGH, N.L.; SEATTLE-TEXAS, A.L. · 1974–82

Mario Mendoza wasn't really a bad hitter. He was terrible. Yet his name lives on in baseball because he left a legacy fit for no other banjo hitter. He gave the game a new statistic that bears his name—the "Mendoza Line." It's now firmly entrenched as part of baseball's jargon, a stigma for all big leaguers to fear and shun.

George Brace Photo

During his brief career, Mendoza had a lifetime average of just .215. When the Rangers released him in 1982, his batting average was so low you needed a magnifying glass to see it—.118.

Mendoza's hitting skills prompted the remark attributed to Kansas City star George Brett that has immortalized Mendoza. "The first thing I look for [in the listing of batting averages] in the Sunday papers is to see who's below the Mendoza Line," Brett said. Thus, the Mendoza Line, the bottom line which no self respecting batter hopes to cross, was born.

The Chicago Cubs

JUNE 15–21, 1968

Leave it to the Cubs to match a 62-year-old record for mass impotency at the plate.

Not since the 1906 Philadelphia Athletics had an entire team's scoring slump been so horrendous. At least the A's had a lame excuse for not scoring runs—pitchers back then could legally throw spitballs and cutballs. The Cubs had no excuse. They equalled the futility record of 48 consecutive scoreless innings and tied another mark for being consecutively shut out in four straight games.

The ignoble slump started June 15 after Chicago had tallied two runs in the first two innings of a 10-inning 3–2 loss to Atlanta. After that, the Cubs belonged on a farm because they collected nothing but goose eggs for days.

The next game the Cubs were blanked by the Braves in 11 innings 1–0. Then the Chicago Flubs dropped three straight to the Cardinals, 1–0, 4–0, and 1–0. They couldn't get a run even if they had worn nylons.

In Cincinnati, they tied the consecutive scoreless innings record in the second inning and looked like a cinch to break the mark. But they had to settle for joint ownership with the A's because charitable Reds pitcher George Culver took pity on Chicago and decided to help. In the third, he walked three Cubs to fill the bases and allowed a sacrifice fly by Billy Williams to snap the unbelievable scoring drought.

Cub pitcher Ferguson Jenkins should have sued his team for nonsupport. During the streak, he pitched eighteen innings and gave up only one run. Yet all he had to show for his stellar pitching was one loss and one no-decision.

Bill Bergen

CINCINNATI-BROOKLYN, N.L. · 1901–11

Bill Bergen's feat has withstood the detest of time. For nearly three-quarters of a century, no regular major leaguer has hit for a worse career batting average.

The great mystery about Bergen is how did the guy manage to last 11 seasons in the bigs with his atrociously weak hitting?

During his career, Bergen played in 947 games, but only once in all that time did he hit above .200. That was in 1903 when he surged to a lofty .227. In all of his 3,028 times at bat, Bergen hit only two home runs. In 1909, he appeared in the most games of his career, 112, and hit an embarrassing .139.

Bergen's miniscule lifetime batting average was just .170. It should actually be lower. During part of his career, walks counted as hits.

George Brace Photo

Joe Torre

THIRD BASEMAN · NEW YORK, N.L. · JULY 21, 1975

Four times Joe Torre came to bat in a game. Four times he grounded into a double play.

No one had ever done that before in the National League, although the dubious feat equaled the American League record held by Goose Goslin of the 1934 Detroit Tigers and Mike Kreevich of the 1939 Chicago White Sox.

However, Torre's batting performance was the most shameful because of what he did to his teammate, second baseman Felix Millan. Hitting ahead of Torre, Millan smacked four straight singles—and all four times Millan found himself sliding into the dirt at second base with umpire Ed Sudol standing over him, thumb pointing skyward.

At the time, Torre was the Met's thirty-five-year-old third baseman and team leader, a lifetime .300 hitter. But try as he might, Torre just could not hit the ball anywhere but on the ground straight at the infielders in a home game against the Houston Astros.

Torre began his assault on the embarrassing record in the first inning with Houston leading 2–0. Millan singled but was wiped out when Torre tapped into a pitcher-to-second-to-first double play. In the third with Houston on top 5–1, the Mets fought back as Del Unser and Millan singled. But the threat was snuffed out when Torre hit an inning-ending double play, short to second to first. In the sixth, the Astros were winning 6–1 when Millan singled. Once again, he was erased when Torre bounced into a second-to-short-to-first twin killing.

Trailing in the eighth 6–2, the Mets launched another rally as Unser and Millan singled. Up came Torre with a chance to redeem himself. Instead, he not only broke the league record but the rally as well by slapping a double-play grounder to short. The Mets, despite collecting eleven hits, lost 6–2.

Since Torre accounted for almost a third of all Mets outs, teammate Tom Seaver offered to hide Joe in a trunk to get him out of the stadium alive after the game.

The following night, Met manager Yogi Berra benched Torre. The Mets won 3–1.

The Rear End of the Front Office

The Most Disgraceful Actions by Owners

Baseball owners and dictators are much alike. They can do what they want because who's going to stop them? The only difference between the two is that owners last longer. There are no armed revolts in baseball. With no one to answer to, owners have pulled off outrageous schemes out of greed, ignorance or nastiness. For "The Most Disgraceful Actions by Owners," The Baseball Hall of SHAME inducts the following:

Walter O'Malley's Abandonment of Brooklyn
1957

There have been some low-down, sneaky tricks perpetrated by owners in the name of money, but none were quite as treacherous, none quite as contemptible as the one committed by Dodger owner Walter Francis O'Malley. He packed up his team and scurried off to Los Angeles—after promising the Brooklyn fans he wouldn't abandon them.

O'Malley had spent most of the 1957 season talking about building a

New York Daily News Photo

new stadium or enlarging Ebbets Field. But it was hollow talk. While piously assuring Brooklyn that he wanted to remain there, he was playing footsie with the city of Los Angeles. Later in the year, O'Malley began talking out of both sides of his mouth about moving and then not moving the Dodgers. But in the end he betrayed the fans.

The bombshell announcement struck on October 8, 1957. A howl of outrage echoed from one end of the borough to the other as fans and local politicians accused O'Malley of double-crossing them. The streets of Flatbush ran wet with tears of anguish and anger. Ebbets Field, the sacred grounds at 215 Montague Street, would no longer bear witness to the beloved Bums.

Philip K. Wrigley's College of Coaches

1961–65

Owners fire managers all the time. But Chicago Cubs owner Phil Wrigley went one better. He *eliminated* managers.

Between 1961 and 1965, the Cubs didn't even have a manager. They had a committee. An eight-member "college of coaches" took turns steering the Cubs in and around the National League cellar. Tired of firing managers, Wrigley conjured up the dumb idea of not hiring any. He decided the club could be run by a group of head coaches who would take turns directing the team at different times during the season.

When he introduced the new system, Wrigley sent out a manual

explaining how the Cubs play baseball. Everybody already knew how the Cubs played—badly. But no one could figure out how the team was going to win without a manager. Wrigley provided an explanation with typical loser logic: "We certainly cannot do much worse trying a new system than we have done for many years under the old."

The original faculty of the "college of coaches" was made up of Rip Collins, Vedie Himsl, Harry Craft, El Tappe, Gordie Holt, Charlie Grimm, Verlon Walker, and Bobby Adams. The Cubs general manager John Holland said these men were chosen because, "We didn't want the type of guy who wants it done his way or else. We needed harmony, men who can be overruled and not take it personally." In other words, the Cub management wanted eight flavors of Jello.

Needless to say, the experiment was a colossal flop. Without firm, consistent leadership, chaos reigned in the dugout. Each time a new head coach took over in the rotation, he brought a different style of play and penned a different lineup. The only thing consistent about the plan was the end result—the Cubs kept losing.

Dan Topping's Firing of Yogi Berra

1964

Despite crippling injuries to the Yankees, first-year manager Yogi Berra guided his wounded team to the pennant. So how did owner Daniel R.

Topping Sr. reward him? By firing him, of course. It was an underhanded plot that eventually left the owner with egg dripping off his face.

Back in July, 1964, the Yankee hierarchy agreed to dump Berra at the end of the season no matter how well the team finished. Meanwhile, an intermediary arranged for St. Louis Cardinal manager Johnny Keane to take over Berra's job for the 1965 season. Only a privileged few were privy to the smelly arrangement which was kept hush-hush to avoid any "lame duck" management problems the Yankees might face if Yogi and the team knew he was on the way out.

As fate would have it, Berra's Yankees and Keane's Cardinals faced each other in the World Series. St. Louis went on to beat New York in seven games.

The next day, Keane announced his resignation and Berra was told to report to the Yankee front office. Expecting to be rehired after overcoming great odds to lead his team to the Series, Berra was shocked—he had been given the boot. The weak excuse spoon-fed to the public was that Berra had no control over his players and couldn't communicate with them. Nobody mentioned that the firing was the end result of long-standing subterfuge.

The deceit came back to haunt the Yankee owner. Keane promptly took the team to where it hadn't been in 40 years—a sixth place finish.

Ray Kroc's Public Scathing of his Team

APRIL 9, 1974

Ray Kroc set a new speed record for losing fans and alienating players.

After only four games as new owner of the San Diego Padres, the hamburger tycoon had a major beef over his team's poor performance on the field. In the eighth inning of the Padres' home opener, he grabbed the public address microphone and loudly lambasted his team while it was losing to the Houston Astros 9–2.

"Ladies and gentlemen, I suffer with you," he told the stunned crowd of 39,083. Kroc's outburst was interrupted by the sudden appearance of a streaker on the field. Since he was nude, no one could tell if he was a Padre or Astro fan. "Get that streaker out of here!" Kroc screamed in the microphone. "Throw him in jail!"

When the comic relief subsided, Kroc returned to his tirade over the Padres. "I've never seen such stupid baseball playing in my life," he declared. Kroc's tantrum had a definite effect on his team that year. They lost 102 games.

Ted Turner's Managing for a Day

MAY 11, 1977

Embarrassing his players and demeaning the game, Braves owner Ted Turner donned a uniform and went down to the dugout to play manager.

The team had already suffered enough, mired in a 16-game losing streak, without becoming reluctant characters in Turner's theater of the absurd. Turner had shipped manager Dave Bristol off on a 10-day "scouting trip," then signed himself to a standard eight-page coach's contract and marched down on the field to run the club.

Turner showed his style when he suited up. First he put on his pants, then the stirrups and socks. Real players do it just the opposite. Rolling their eyes in dismay, the players cringed at the thought of what would happen next.

One of the regular coaches jotted down the lineup card for Turner and the boss signed it "R.E. Turner." As expected, Turner's managerial debut was a bust. The Braves lost their seventeenth straight by a score of 2–1.

The next day, Turner was ready to try managing again. But National League president Chub Feeney found a rule that says managers or players cannot own any financial interest in a club. When Feeney told Turner to get out of uniform and back in the stands where he belonged, Turner whimpered, "Can't I do what I want to?" He went trudging off, whining, "I wish I could hit somebody, but there's nobody to hit."

Later that day while sitting in the stands, Turner discussed his managerial philosophy: "Managing isn't all that difficult. Just score more runs than the other guy."

Jacob Ruppert's Dumping of Babe Ruth

FALL, 1934

Old Jake the brewmeister left a stain on baseball that all the apologizing in the world couldn't wipe away.

Ruppert might be remembered by many as the owner who built the Yankee dynasty of the 1920s. But that doesn't excuse the insulting manner in which he dumped Babe Ruth.

As an active player whose career was drawing to a close, the thirty-nine-year-old Ruth had his heart set on managing. He didn't want to pilot any team. He wanted to manage the Yankees, his heart and soul for 15 years.

But Ruppert was a classic aristocrat who detested the same hired help that made him rich and famous. He disdainfully told "Root," as he called

George Brace Photo

41

the home run king, that the Yankees might find a slot for a has-been like him in their minor league system. Maybe Newark for starters. Ruth was crushed and offended by the snub and at the end of the 1934 season, he went off on a barnstorming tour of the Far East.

Meanwhile, Ruppert and general manager Ed Barrow concocted a scheme to get rid of the star who had made the Yankees a baseball institution. When Ruth returned home, they sprang their nasty plot.

Ruppert offered the great Bambino one lousy dollar to play the 1935 season unless Ruth proved worthy of more after spring training. Not even the bat boy could accept such audacious terms and Ruth was driven to end his playing career with the lowly Boston Braves.

Blind Spots

The Most Flagrant Blown Calls by Umpires

Umpires are necessary evils like batting slumps, bad-hop singles, and cold hot dogs. Without them, what would fans have to complain about? Grudgingly, fans must admit that umpires are pretty honest fellows. It's just that the men in blue aren't always right. You'd swear that some of their calls were made while using a red-tipped cane. For "The Most Flagrant Blown Calls by Umpires," The Baseball Hall of SHAME inducts the following:

Ken Burkhart's Behind-the-Back Call

OCT. 10, 1970

Umpire Ken Burkhart violated a cardinal rule—never get caught out of position. As a result, he made a horrendous call at the plate on a crucial play that took place behind his back in the 1970 World Series.

Burkhart's infamous moment came in the sixth inning of the first game with the Baltimore Orioles leading the Cincinnati Reds 4–3. The Reds Bernie Carbo was at third when Ty Cline hit a high chopper in front of the plate. Orioles catcher Elrod Hendricks jumped out to field it while Burkhart straddled the third base line to call the ball fair or foul. Unfortunately, the ump ignored Carbo who was barreling down the third base line for home.

With Burkhart blocking the plate, Carbo tried to hook slide around the umpire. By now Hendricks, who had fielded the ball, lunged at Carbo in an attempt to make the tag and collided with Burkhart. The only guy

in the entire stadium who couldn't clearly see what was happening was Burkhart. But even though his back was to the play, he called Carbo out.

Instant replays and sequence photos revealed that Hendricks had indeed tagged Carbo—but with an empty glove while holding the ball with his throwing hand. The replays and photos also showed that Carbo slid wide of the plate—and touched it safely only by accident when he returned to protest the call.

Burkhart's decision was a crucial mistake because the Reds lost the game 4–3, and eventually the Series.

George Hildebrand's Stopping of the Game

OCT. 5, 1922

The tension during the second game of the 1922 World Series was almost unbearable. After ten heart-thumping innings between the Giants and the Yankees, the score was deadlocked 3–3. The fans couldn't wait to see what would happen next. Unfortunately, the fans couldn't *get* to see what would happen next.

Umpire George Hildebrand took the ball from the catcher, stuck it in his pocket and announced the game was called "on account of darkness." Then he marched off the unlighted field.

The players, fans, even Commissioner Kenesaw Mountain Landis couldn't believe their ears. It was still a bright, sunny October afternoon, about 4:45 P.M. There was at least another 45 minutes of playing time left.

When fans realized that one of the most thrilling games they had ever seen was over without a winner, they exploded in anger. The umpires ran for their lives as a mob poured out onto the field and surrounded Landis, who was just as upset as the furious fans.

Screaming "Fraud!" they demanded their money back and pelted the commissioner with curses and bottles as he pushed and shoved his way to the umpires' locked and guarded dressing room.

"Why in the Sam Hill did you call the game?" he thundered at Hildebrand.

"There was a temporary haze on the field," the ump replied. The only haze seemed to be in Hildebrand's thinking.

To appease the angry mob. Landis ordered that receipts from the game—$120,554—be turned over to charity. In private, he read the riot act to Hildebrand about being too quick to call a game.

Wouldn't you know that the next game was played on a drizzly day so dark the players had trouble seeing the ball. But no ump dared call the game.

Larry Barnett's Interference Ruling

OCT. 14, 1975

The enraged Red Sox called Larry Barnett's decision a miscarriage of justice. Actually, they called it many other things that would have made a drill sergeant blush. His ruling certainly rates as one of the most unfair calls in Series history. It came during the third game of the 1975 World Series.

A late rally by Boston had tied Cincinnati 5–5, forcing the game into extra innings. In the bottom of the tenth, Cincy's Cesar Geronimo singled. That brought up Ed Armbrister, an obscure player who was now faced with the most important task of his brief career—move Geronimo into scoring position.

AP/Wide World Photo

He dropped a terrible bunt in front of the plate and it looked like Boston catcher Carlton Fisk had an easy force play at second. As Fisk moved out and picked up the ball, Armbrister hesitated and then placed a nifty NFL shoulder block into Fisk's chest. The two bumped and pushed until, in desperation, Fisk leaped high in the air and threw to second. But because of the jostling with Armbrister, Fisk's throw sailed into center field while Armbrister finally decided to go look for first base. The runners ended up on second and third.

The Red Sox yelled interference loud enough to be heard back in Scully Square, but Barnett wouldn't have any of it. Interference, he said, had to be intentional and Armbrister really didn't mean to get into Fisk's way.

A few moments later, Joe Morgan stroked a single to drive in Geronimo with the winning run and the Reds went on to take the Series in seven games. Moments after the bitter third-game defeat, Fisk raged, "We should have had a double play on that ball, but the umpires are too gutless under pressure."

Vic Delmore's Mental Lapse

JUNE 30, 1959

Because of Vic Delmore's absentmindedness, he caused one of the most bizarre, inexcusable plays in baseball.

It happened in Wrigley Field (where else?). The Cardinals' Stan Musial was at bat with a 3–1 count when the next pitch got away from Cub catcher Sammy Taylor and rolled toward the backstop.

Delmore called ball four and Musial trotted toward first. But Taylor and pitcher Bob Anderson argued that it was a foul tip.

Since the ball was still in play, Musial ran towards second. Quick-thinking third baseman Alvin Dark then ran to the backstop and retrieved the ball. Meanwhile, Delmore was still arguing with the Cub battery mates when he unthinkingly pulled a second ball out of his pocket and handed it to Taylor. Suddenly noticing Musial heading for second, Anderson grabbed the new ball and threw to second—at the same time Dark threw to shortstop Ernie Banks with the original ball.

Anderson's throw sailed over second base into center field. Musial saw the ball fly past his head, so—not knowing there were two balls in play—he took off for third only to run right into Banks who tagged him out with the original ball.

After a lengthy huddle, the umpires ruled that Musial was out since he was tagged with the original ball. Also "out" was Vic Delmore. Citing a "lack of confidence," National League President Warren Giles fired Delmore at the end of the season.

All Choked Up

The Teams That Blew the Biggest Leads and Lost

One of baseball's favorite images is of the underdog team that dramatically overcomes incredible odds, and, with superhuman effort, comes from behind at the last possible moment to win a game or pennant. That's all bunk. The other team just blew it, plain and simple. The losers' logo should depict two hands firmly clutching the throat. For "The Teams That Blew the Biggest Leads and Lost," The Baseball Hall of SHAME inducts the following:

The Philadelphia Phillies

1964

The word "choke" was invented in Philadelphia late in September, 1964, when the Phillies suffered one of the most awesome collapses in modern times.

Owning a 6½-game lead with only 15 games to play, the Phillies could have waltzed to the pennant without so much as breaking a sweat. Instead, they dropped ten straight and while they staggered to get back on their feet, the St. Louis Cardinals stepped over them to claim the pennant.

What was so amazing about the famous Phillies flop, which began September 18, was that it was a total team effort. Everything went to pieces at the same time—hitting, pitching, defense, even managing.

For instance, skipper Gene Mauch drew a lot of heat for overworking to exhaustion his two aces, Jim Bunning (19–8) and Chris Short (17–9). Three times in September he sent Bunning to the mound with only two days rest. He did the same thing with Short. The pitching duo lost all those games they appeared in during that stretch.

Then there were the defensive lapses. Twice they lost because they allowed base runners to steal home. In another dreadful game against the Braves, outfielder Johnny Callison let a fly ball bounce off his glove, allowing the winning run to score. Also in that game, the Phils Richie Allen overslid second and was tagged out when he didn't even try to get back to the bag. And teammate Alex Johnson immediately followed that base-running blunder with one of his own when he rounded second base and was picked off.

The Phillies won their last game of the season against the Reds and salvaged a second place tie with Cincinnati, just one game out of first. They came so close. But close counts only in horseshoes.

National League Standings of Sept. 18, 1964

	W	L	Pct	GB
Philadelphia	89	58	.605	—
St. Louis	82	64	.562	6½
Cincinnati	81	65	.555	7½
San Francisco	81	66	.551	8
Pittsburgh	75	70	.517	13
Milwaukee	75	71	.514	13½
Los Angeles	73	74	.497	16
Chicago	66	80	.452	22½
Houston	60	88	.405	29½
New York	50	96	.342	38½

Final National League Standings of 1964

	W	L	Pct	GB
St. Louis	93	69	.574	—
Cincinnati	92	70	.568	1
Philadelphia	92	70	.568	1
San Francisco	90	72	.556	3
Milwaukee	88	74	.543	5
Los Angeles	80	82	.494	13
Pittsburgh	80	82	.494	13
Chicago	76	86	.469	17
Houston	66	96	.407	27
New York	53	109	.327	40

The Washington Senators

MAY 23, 1901

It was the last of the ninth in a real yawner. The Senators were way out in front of the Cleveland Blues (later named the Indians) by a score of 13–5 with two out.

Most of the bored, disillusioned fans had set out for home. The Senators were one out away from victory and ready for their showers. But they ended up taking a bath.

The Senators bat boy was packing up the equipment as pitcher Case Patten bore down on what he thought would be the last batter. But unbelievably, that third out was as elusive as a greased pig. In fact, the Senators never did get that final out.

Washington pitchers proceeded to give up six singles, two doubles, a walk, a hit batsman, and a passed ball. That added up to nine runs! The Senators' 13–5 lead turned into a 14–13 loss.

The Boston Red Sox

1978

After the debacle of the 1978 season, the Red Sox belonged not in Boston but in Choke City.

On July 21, first place Boston was so far ahead of New York (13½ games) that the Yankees needed binoculars to see the Red Sox. No one could catch them, said most everyone in baseball.

After all, on this team were talented All-Stars like Carl Yastrzemski, Fred Lynn, Jim Rice, Carlton Fisk, George Scott, and Dwight Evans. The pitching staff was headed by Mike Torrez, Luis Tiant, Bill Lee, and Dennis Eckersley. How could such a strong team lose? That's a question baseball historians are still trying to figure out.

The Red Sox were flying high throughout the first half of the year but suddenly they stalled in the rarefied air at the top of the standings and plummeted earthward, losing nine of ten at the end of July. Somehow they recovered and built up an 8½ game lead by August 20.

But then they totally collapsed, dropping 14 of 17 games from August 30 through September 16. Torrez, once 15–6, lost seven of his last eight decisions. Tiant went through a stretch when he dropped seven of nine games. Lee lost his final seven decisions.

Smack-dab in the tailspin, the Red Sox were clinging desperately to a four-game lead when they faced the Yankees at Fenway Park in early September. A sweep by Boston would just about guarantee the team the pennant. Instead the Red Sox were hung out to dry in a sweep of the series by the Yanks. First place was no longer the Beantowners' private residence. As the slump continued, they were booted out of first and stumbled 3½ games behind New York before they finally were revived from their swoon and scrambled to tie the Yankees at the end of the regular season.

Boston had one more chance to redeem itself from a disgraceful collapse—by beating the Yankees in a one-game playoff for the pennant. But the Red Sox blew that game too, losing 5–4.

"Our pain isn't as bad as you might think," said Bill Lee. "Dead bodies don't suffer."

American League Standings
of July 21, 1978

EASTERN DIVISION	W	L	Pct	GB
Boston	62	28	.689	—
Milwaukee	53	37	.589	9
Baltimore	51	42	.548	12½
New York	49	42	.538	13½
Detroit	46	45	.505	16½
Cleveland	43	49	.467	20
Toronto	33	59	.359	30

Final American League Standings
of 1978

EASTERN DIVISION	W	L	Pct	GB
New York	100	63	.613	—
Boston	99	64	.607	1
Milwaukee	93	69	.574	6½
Baltimore	90	71	.559	9
Detroit	86	76	.531	13½
Cleveland	69	90	.434	29
Toronto	59	102	.366	40

Bubble Gum Bozos

The Most Unprofessional Baseball Cards

Somewhere in those stacks of baseball cards, there's a misfit to suit every taste—poor taste, that is. The bubbleheaded poses some players have gotten away with should be in a rogues' gallery instead of a bubble gum card collection. And the companies who deal these cards have been caught in more than one fast shuffle themselves. For "The Most Unprofessional Baseball Cards," The Baseball Hall of SHAME inducts the following:

Billy Martin
MANAGER · DETROIT, A.L. · 1972

If ever there was a wild card in the deck of trading cards, you can bet it was Billy's. He sneaked one over on the Topps bubble gum people.

As the manager of the Detroit Tigers at the time and supposedly a leader of men, Billy was asked to pose like a very serious-minded field general for card number 33.

He did, all right. But he added one extra touch that spoke a lot about his character. He leaned on his bat and extended his middle finger down the handle in a subtle but nonetheless graphic display of the classic obscene-finger gesture.

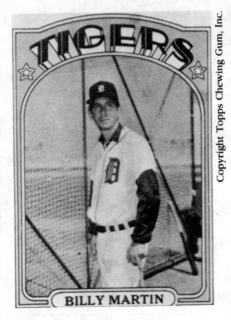

BILLY MARTIN

AURELIO RODRIGUEZ 3rd Base

ANGELS

Aurelio Rodriguez

THIRD BASEMAN · CALIFORNIA, A.L. · 1969

Although he would later rise to prominence as a slick fielder, Aurelio Rodriguez was a virtual unknown in 1969. *How* unknown became apparent after the nifty trick he pulled on Topps' card number 653.

Urged by his California teammates, Rodriguez switched uniforms with someone else. As a result, the Topps photographer shot the wrong person. The guy in the Angels uniform that the baseball card identified as Rodriguez was really Leonard Garcia—a 16-year-old bat boy!

Jay Johnstone

OUTFIELDER · CHICAGO, N.L. · 1984

When Fleer came out with its 1984 edition, every kid in America suddenly had a new role model for shame—one who wore silly hats promoting beer drinking.

During his outfielding career with eight major league clubs, Jay Johnstone carried with him a reputation for first class flakiness. To prove that this flake was no fluke, Johnstone posed for card number 495 wearing a Budweiser umbrella hat. This confirmed suspicions from his teammates that he doesn't always play with a full deck.

Duane Kuiper

SECOND BASEMAN · SAN FRANCISCO, N.L. · 1983

There's a joker dealt every spring when players pose for baseball cards. Kuiper was it in 1983.

On Fleer's card number 263, he looked the part of a big league player. But his pose was strictly bush league. He was photographed holding the fat end of the bat which had a broken handle hanging by a splinter and dangling over his shoulder.

If that's typical of the way the Giant batters come to the plate, it explains why the team hasn't made it to the World Series since 1962.

Topps Bubble Gum Co.

1966

There was nothing funny about the colossal goof by Topps in 1966 that embarrassed everyone associated with major league baseball.

Topps' card number 447 featured the brief biography and lifetime statistics of Dick Ellsworth, a pitcher for the Chicago Cubs.

But the picture they used on the front of the card was that of infielder Ken Hubbs. Tragically, Hubbs had been killed in a plane crash two years earlier.

DICK ELLSWORTH   pitcher

Copyright Topps Chewing Gum, Inc.

The Blights of Spring

The Most Outrageous Behavior in Spring Training

Springtime, and a young man's thoughts turn to things rowdy and riotous—especially if he's in the major leagues. Don't be fooled by the phony image of spring training as a camp for the clean-living and high-minded to work out the winter kinks. More often, it's a time for disgraceful shenanigans and fracases that bring out the worst in players. For "The Most Outrageous Behavior in Spring Training," The Baseball Hall of SHAME inducts the following:

The New York Giants
SPRING, 1904

Some major league clubs were about as welcome at the spring training sites as a swarm of locusts. The Giants in the early part of the century were among the worst of the lot when it came to making friends and influencing the home folks in Alabama where the team trained.

Under manager John J. McGraw, the Giants became particularly adept at lathering up the local vigilantes into fits of righteous wrath at the mere mention of baseball. The fact that these were mainly northern boys did not set well in southern cities. Besides, the players tended to be a louty, boastful bunch who strutted around town with money in their pockets and the Flower of Southern Womanhood at their heels, a condition guaranteed to put the local youth severely out of joint.

The team was ordered out of its spring training home of Birmingham, Alabama, after a New York writer traveling with the Giants wrote that the city was a jerk-water little town where the big excitement was watching mold grow. The unflattering picture angered the mayor of Birmingham enough to insist McGraw make the reporter retract the defamatory article. In his rather graphic language, McGraw told His Honor where he could stick his objection. And the Mayor told McGraw where he could shove his Giants—namely, the hell out of Birmingham.

In Mobile, the Giants firmed up their reputation as "The Team Most Likely to Be Invited to its Own Lynching." During a rough-house exhibition game, McGraw's men, never known for their restraint, proceeded to beat into unconsciousness the hometown umpire whose officiating was about as smelly as a week-old catfish on an Alabama mudflat in August. The Mobilians were not at all pleased. Warrants for the arrest of all the Giants were sworn out forthwith. Just about everybody above the age of toddler volunteered to join the posse to go after the Giants. For once, McGraw showed good sense. He packed up the team and beat it out of town before sundown.

Dizzy Dean

PITCHER · ST. LOUIS, N.L. · SPRING, 1934

Nobody detested batters more than Dizzy. Show him a guy with a bat in his hand and Diz would foam at the mouth. And pity the poor batter who dared dig in against him. Dizzy would yell: "You all done? You comfortable? Well, send for the groundskeeper and get a shovel 'cause that's where they're gonna bury you." The hitter would then be diving in the dirt with the next pitch.

Diz served notice that even in spring training he wouldn't tolerate such foolishness as batters getting hits off him. During an exhibition game in Miami, the Giants insulted Dizzy by scoring seven runs in one inning. They should have known better. Stomping and snarling on the mound, Diz went to work getting even. He plunked the next seven Giant batters in a row.

Only then did the umpire stop the mayhem by ordering Cardinal manager Frankie Frisch to get "that maniac" off the mound. It was, after all, only spring training.

George Harper

OUTFIELDER · CINCINNATI, N.L. · SPRING, 1922

George Harper shamed the name of hitters everywhere when he slunk back to the dugout even though he hadn't finished taking his turn at bat.

Harper was with the Reds when they met the Senators in Tampa. For many of the Cincinnati players, it was their first up close look at fireballing pitcher Walter Johnson. For some it was too close. Even though it was toward the end of his career, Johnson's fastball was still a fearsome thing for the fainthearted at the plate to behold. Harper was among the faintest of the faint.

The first time he went up to hit against Johnson he didn't even get the bat off his shoulder. The ball whizzed by Harper as umpire Bill Klem called, "Strike one!" Harper stepped out of the batter's box, shook his head in amazement and then moved back in his stance. Harper had hardly planted his feet when another pitch whizzed past him and Klem hollered, "Strike two!" That was enough. Harper turned and walked back to the dugout.

"Wait," Klem said. "You still have one strike left."

"I don't want it," the white-faced Harper answered. He headed straight for the safety of the dugout.

Lenny Randle

SECOND BASEMAN · TEXAS, A.L. · MARCH 28, 1977

Pranks and practical jokes are part of spring training lore, but there was nothing funny in the way Randle responded to being benched by Ranger manager Frank Lucchesi. Out on the street it's called a mugging.

At twenty-eight, Randle was an athlete in peak condition. He had been the Rangers regular second baseman, but he slumped to a weak .224 during the 1976 season. When spring training rolled around Randle was benched for his lackluster play. His chronic complaints about being demoted finally got to his manager. Lucchesi told reporters, "I'm tired of these punks saying 'Play me or trade me.' Anyone who makes eighty thousand dollars a year and gripes and moans all spring is not going to get a tear out of me."

What Randle got out of Lucchesi was a lot of blood when he confronted the 50-year-old manager behind the batting cage in Orlando. Randle said Lucchesi called him a punk again. Lucchesi said he was merely standing there with his hands in his pockets when Randle, who had had some training in martial arts, started punching. Witnesses said at least three, maybe more, blows landed and Lucchesi went to the hospital with a shattered right cheekbone that required plastic surgery.

Randle was charged with aggravated battery, a felony that could have put him in the slammer for 15 years. Later, he plea-bargained to a reduced charge of simple battery. He was fined $1,000 and ordered to pay Lucchesi's medical expenses. The Rangers also fined Randle $10,000 and suspended him for a month. He was then released and quickly signed by the Mets, who were trying to get some "punch" in their lineup.

Take Me Out to the Brawl Game

The Most Flagrant Cases of Assault and Battery on the Field

Baseball players can hit but few can fight. A typical fracas between teams looks more like a 50-percent-off sale at Macy's—lots of shoving, a little scuffling and some harsh words. But every now and then, the baseball field takes on the ugly specter of street-gang warfare. Players wield bats to bash heads, not baseballs. They throw punches rather than pitches. For "The Most Flagrant Cases of Assault and Battery on the Field," The Baseball Hall of SHAME inducts the following:

Juan Marichal

PITCHER · SAN FRANCISCO, N.L. · AUG. 22, 1965

Dodgers catcher John Roseboro lay in the dust, dazed and bleeding from a horrible gash on the top of his head. His assailant, Juan Marichal, had just struck him with a bat. It was one of the sorriest sights ever seen in a baseball game.

As usual, there had been bad blood between the Giants and the Dodgers, who had been battling for first place throughout the 1965 season. During the first two games of a three-game series at Candlestick Park, the teams exchanged charges of interference and brush-back pitches. By the third

game, antagonism between the two clubs had reached a fever pitch.

Giants ace Juan Marichal, 19–9 at the time, dueled Sandy Koufax, 21–4. In the bottom of the third inning, with the Dodgers ahead 2–1, Marichal came to bat and took a few swings at contemptibility.

After taking two inside pitches, he stepped back and then, without a word, suddenly unleashed a vicious attack, clubbing Roseboro over the head several times. Roseboro crumbled to the ground unable to protect himself. A howl of outrage ripped through the stands and both benches emptied onto the field. Players and coaches rushed in to save Roseboro from being beaten to death.

The berserk Marichal ran down toward first base, the bat now a lethal club in his hands. Members from both teams tried to surround him and get the bat away, but no one dared get too close. When Marichal was distracted by one of the players, umpire Shag Crawford leaped in and grabbed him. Both fell to the ground as others piled on.

While Marichal was dragged off the field, Roseboro was rushed to the hospital and treated for a two-inch gash on his head. To prevent further trouble, San Francisco police stood in front of the stands from foul pole to foul pole as the shaken players completed the game, won by the Giants 4–3.

In his unacceptable excuse, Marichal said he had been provoked because he had been nicked on the ear by one of Roseboro's return throws to Koufax. It was the first time in recent memory when a catcher was accused of throwing at a pitcher.

National League President Warren Giles didn't buy Marichal's excuse. In a telegram to the pitcher, Giles stated: "I am sure you recognize how repugnant your actions were in the game. Such actions are harmful to the game and must be dealt with drastically ... Your sudden and violent action was unprovoked and obnoxious and must be penalized."

However, Giles' so-called drastic punishment was nothing more than a slap on the wrist—a $1,750 fine and a nine-day suspension. The sentence outraged the Dodgers, especially Ron Fairly, who declared, "That's sickening. It should be a suspension of 1,750 days."

The punishment hurt the Giants more than anyone thought. Marichal was forced to miss two starting assignments because of the suspension and when he returned he was relatively ineffective. As a result, the Giants lost the pennant to the Dodgers by a slim two-game margin.

Billy Martin

SECOND BASEMAN · CINCINNATI, N.L. · AUG. 4, 1960

One of the cheapest sucker punches ever thrown was delivered by Billy Martin when he slugged Cub pitcher Jim Brewer during a game at Wrigley Field.

In the second inning, Martin blew up over what he thought was a brush-back pitch. He took the next pitch and as soon as the ball hit the

AP/Wide World Photo

catcher's glove, Martin threw his bat at Brewer. (Later, Martin claimed that the bat "slipped out of my hands.")

Brewer picked up the bat and held it out to give it to Martin, who was approaching the mound. Recalled Brewer, "When he walked out there, all he said was, 'I'm just coming after my bat, kid.' And before I knew what happened, I was hit with a Sunday punch."

Martin uncorked a right-handed shot that shattered Brewer's right cheekbone and depressed the eyeball socket bone by half an inch below Brewer's right eye. The injury was serious enough to require two months of hospitalization and two reconstructive operations to repair the damage. Martin, who had been ejected from the game, received a shockingly mild five-day suspension and a $500 fine.

The Cubs subsequently sued Martin for $1 million for the loss of Brewer's services. When informed of the suit, Martin sarcastically cracked, "How do they want it? In cash or check?"

That suit was dropped but Brewer pursued his own case in court. It took nine years to resolve. The judge ordered Martin to pay Brewer $10,000 for damages.

Pittsburgh Pirates vs. Los Angeles Dodgers
AUG. 25, 1981

What made this fight between teams so shameful was that it took place under the stands in private—in the middle of the game—while the fans wondered where everyone went.

The main event featured Pirates' rookie pitcher Pascual Perez and the Dodgers' Reggie Smith. From the dugout, Smith, who was out with an injury, began shouting at Perez that he was throwing too many pitches high and inside at the Dodgers.

No doubt, Perez was doing just that. Only he threw a little too tight in the sixth inning and clipped Bill Russell on the hand. When another pitch hit Dusty Baker, Perez received a warning from umpire Dutch Rennert.

While that discussion was going on, Pirate third baseman Bill Madlock traded words and gestures with Smith. "If you want to fight, pick on me, not Perez," Madlock shouted to Smith.

Perez didn't want any stand-in. When the inning ended, Perez yelled at Smith to meet him under the stands, then raced through the Pirates dugout, pausing long enough to grab a bat.

The Pirates followed Perez into the runway leading to the common hall under the stands. Meanwhile, the Dodgers cleared out of their dugout and ran behind Smith. Since no one was on the field, the umpires left, too, looking for the fight scene.

The bewildered 16,000-plus fans wondered where all the action was. It was taking place under the stands, where a pushing, shoving, shouting bunch of players, managers, coaches and trainers were mixing it up (without hurting anybody). After five minutes, the umpires prevailed without resorting to any ejections. All the bruised, pampered and high-priced egos had been soothed and the players returned to the field where they belonged.

Carl Furillo

OUTFIELDER · BROOKLYN, N.L. · SEPT. 6, 1953

Carl Furillo, wearing Dodger blue, charged into the Giants dugout all by himself to pick a fight with manager Leo Durocher, who was surrounded by Giants. Now is that dumb or is that dumb?

New York was playing Brooklyn at Ebbets Field and needless to say there was no love lost between the two teams. Ever since 1948 when Leo had switched allegiances and gone from managing the Dodgers to taking over the reins of the Giants, Durocher, in the eyes of the Bums, was responsible for all the evils in the world.

During the game, Furillo, wielding the hottest bat in the league, heard Durocher's shrill voice from the dugout screaming to Giants pitcher Ruben Gomez to "stick it in his ear," a favorite Leoism. On the very next pitch, Furillo was popped on the posterior by a Gomez fast ball.

Rubbing at the soreness and fuming as he trotted down to first base, Furillo glared at the grinning Durocher. "I'll get you for that!" shouted Furillo.

"Here I am," Durocher snorted back.

With that invitation, Furillo leaped into the Giants dugout with only one thing on his mind—bare-handed strangulation. Instead, he disappeared under a mound of delighted Giants who happily stomped Furillo into a pulp. When the Dodgers finally dug him out, Furillo staggered away with a broken bone in his left hand that kept him out of the lineup for the rest of the season.

It was a painful lesson for anyone foolish enough to go into the enemy's dugout alone. Furillo didn't even get the satisfaction of busting his hand on Durocher's nose.

One good thing happened out of this melee. Since Furillo was through for the year, he didn't have to risk lowering his league-leading batting average of .344. As a result, he won the crown by two percentage points. It was the first time a player ever won the batting title with the help of getting hit in the ass.

Atlanta vs. San Diego

AUG. 12, 1984

A little chin music, maestro, and we'll all dance the Brush-Back polka viciously brought your way by those two wonderful sportsmen, Joe Torre and Dick Williams, and their infamous "Stick It in Your Ear" band!

The two managers orchestrated one of the worst beanball wars in modern times and it cost their teams dearly—to the tune of 13 ejections.

That's not all. At least five fans were dragged out of Atlanta's Fulton County Stadium in handcuffs for jumping into the brawl on the field. One of the thugs was charged with assault when he threw a full beer mug that caught the Padres' Kurt Bevacqua square on the head when he was returning to the dugout. The game ended with police riot squads stationed on top of both dugouts.

The disgrace started on the first pitch when Atlanta's Pascual Perez drilled Alan Wiggins, who had tormented the Braves the night before with two bunt singles and a stolen base.

Padres pitcher Ed Whitson waited for Perez to bat in the second and then sailed a pitch behind Perez's head in obvious retaliation. Perez made a threatening motion towards the mound, and both teams, already keyed for trouble, emptied onto the field. But there was no fight then. Perhaps if Whitson had only been able to plunk Perez the first time, the insanity that followed wouldn't have happened.

In the fourth inning, a high inside pitch from Whitson sent Perez sprawling. Whitson was ejected for throwing the pitch and manager Dick Williams was thumbed for ordering it.

Greg Booker came in to replace Whitson and coach Ozzie Virgil took Williams' place in the dugout. Still, the Padres didn't feel the score was settled. Perez hadn't been hit yet. They got another chance in the fifth inning when Perez came to the plate again. Booker tried, but his beanball, like the others, missed Perez. And both Booker and Virgil were given the old heave-ho. Nobody questioned the meanness of the Padres pitching staff but fans did start to wonder about their accuracy.

Finally, in the eighth, when by any logic Perez should have been sitting on the bench, Torre sent him up again. It was like waving a very red flag in front of a very enraged bull. Craig Lefferts was pitching now and he finally nailed Perez with the get-even beaner. Naturally, it ignited an all-out fight. The Braves and Padres slugged, punched, and kicked each other in the middle of the field for a good ten minutes before the umpires could restore some order. The game resumed without Lefferts and also coach Jack Krol who had taken over for the ejected Virgil. In from the bullpen came coach Harry Dunlop, who became the Padres' fourth manager of the game.

Now it was the Braves' turn to pour gasoline on the fire. In the ninth inning, relief pitcher Donnie Moore hit Graig Nettles with a pitch. And once more both benches came storming onto the field.

When it was all over, National League President Chub Feeney suspended Padres Champ Summers and Bobby Brown and Braves Gerald Perry, Steve Bedrosian, and Rick Mahler for three days and issued them various fines. He also fined Moore and Perez $350 and $300, respectively. The Padres' fines were not disclosed. Torre drew a three-day suspension and a $1,000 fine. Williams got the stiffest penalty—a ten-day suspension and a $10,000 fine.

Said umpire John McSherry: "It took baseball down fifty years. It was the worst thing I have ever seen in my life. It was pathetic, absolutely pathetic."

Hanging Curves

The Most Pitiful Pitching Performances

You can always spot the lousy pitchers. Their curves hang longer than punts while their fastballs move slower than balloons on a still day. Nevertheless, they play an important role in baseball— they fatten batting averages. For "The Most Pitiful Pitching Performances," The Baseball Hall of SHAME inducts the following:

Paul Foytack

LOS ANGELES, A.L. · JULY 31, 1963

The fans like to see home runs, so Paul Foytack generously obliged—and ended up in the record books.

In the previous ten years in the majors, Foytack had never distinguished himself as anything other than a .500 pitcher. But on this day, in the span of five minutes, he etched his name in the annals of baseball for all to see.

With his team trailing 5–1, the veteran right-hander strode to the mound to face the Cleveland Indians in the sixth inning—and threw pitches that belonged in batting practice.

First, Woody Held smashed a Foytack pitch for a home run. Up to the plate stepped pitcher Pedro Ramos, who sported a paltry .109 batting average that year. He teed off on one of Foytack's servings and belted it for another homer. Then it was Tito Francona's turn. No sooner had he settled into the batter's box than he socked a Foytack pitch for the third consecutive home run. By now, the next batter, rookie Larry Brown, who had yet to hit a major league homer, couldn't wait to swing his bat. Sure enough, Foytack threw him a fat pitch and Brown swatted it over the left field wall for his very first round-tripper.

Scratching his head in disbelief, Angels manager Bill Rigney walked out to the mound—a little too late—and sent the shellshocked Foytack to the showers.

Holding the record for the most consecutive home runs allowed in one inning, Foytack told reporters later, "You may not believe this, but I was trying to knock him (Larry Brown) down with the pitch. That shows you what kind of control I had."

Jack Chesbro

NEW YORK, A.L. · OCT. 10, 1904

Happy Jack Chesbro ended up a Sad Sack after throwing the most disastrous wild pitch in baseball history.

In 1904, Chesbro had pitched phenomenally, winning 41 games to set a record that has never been threatened. On the strength of his arm, his team, the New York Highlanders (now the Yankees), fought the Boston Pilgrims (now the Red Sox) down to the wire for the pennant that year.

On the last day of the season, New York trailed Boston by a single game but the Highlanders could capture the pennant with a double-header sweep over the Pilgrims. With Chesbro getting the call in that first critical game, the New York fans had good reason to hope for a pennant. About 30,000 rooters were on hand, an astonishing number for those days.

The game was a nail-biter and the two teams entered the ninth tied at 2–2. Chesbro got two outs but had a runner on third. He desperately wanted that final out of the inning so he did what he always did in a jam. He went to his spitter.

George Brace Photo

But the pitch that had brought him so many victories that season betrayed him in the end. He threw the wettest and wildest pitch of his career. Catcher Red Kleinow leaped for the ball but it sailed past him and headed for infamy. Boston's runner Lou Criger scampered home with the winning run as a collective moan of despair swept through the stunned crowd. The Highlanders weren't able to score in the last of the ninth and Boston captured the pennant.

Chesbro never seemed to recover from the calamitous pitch. His pitching went downhill after that and he spent the rest of his career trying to keep his hands dry.

Robin Roberts

PHILADELPHIA, N.L. · JULY 18, 1948

Robin Roberts won 286 games in his 19-year career. He would have won 287 but he found a unique and mortifying way to lose a game in his first year in the bigs.

Roberts, then a twenty-one-year-old rookie, had pitched eight strong innings against the Chicago Cubs in Wrigley Field and headed into the bottom of the ninth with the score tied 2–2. The Cubs quickly put runners on first and second but Roberts bore down and got the next two outs.

Then came his moment of shame. He pitched as though he couldn't tell the difference between home plate and a batter's backside. Phil Cavarretta stepped up to bat and Roberts' first pitch hit him right in the back.

That loaded the bases and brought up Andy Pafko. Roberts was determined to get this batter. He did too. Roberts' first pitch to Pafko drilled him smack in the back.

Two successive pitches. Two hit batters. End of game. The HBP forced in the winning run ... and forced Robin Roberts to walk off the mound in humiliation.

Terry Felton

MINNESOTA, A.L. · 1979–82

Terry Felton lost more games at the start of his big league career than any other pitcher in history. He dropped 16 straight games. Even worse, he appeared in 55 games and never once recorded a victory.

Felton was a twenty-one-year-old right-handed hurler for the Minnesota Twins when he first toed the rubber in the bigs on Sept. 28, 1979. Statistics-wise, it was his best season. He pitched two scoreless, hitless innings.

The following year, Felton began his skid toward an inglorious record that had stood unchallenged since 1914 when Cleveland Indians pitcher Guy Morton lost 13 straight before winning his first major league game.

In a span of ten days beginning on April 18, 1980, Felton lost to the Seattle Mariners 3–2, was bombed by the California Angels 17–0 and fell to Seattle again, 6–4. It finally dawned on the Twins front office that maybe this guy needed a little more seasoning in the minors, so Felton was shipped to the Toledo Mud Hens in the International League.

He returned to the majors in 1981 and pitched one inning. That was more than enough. He gave up four runs, six hits and two walks.

Refusing to believe he was as bad as he looked, the Twins used Felton in 48 games in 1982. He specialized in relief pitching—and in throwing home run pitches. In his first 100 innings of the season, he served up 18 homers—including five game-losers that broke ties in the seventh inning or later.

"God's got something in for me, I reckon," Felton told reporters. "He's supposed to be on the underdog's side, right? I keep throwing mistakes and every time I do that they hit it. I think I've got a snake around my neck, biting me every time I'm out there."

Things got so desperate that Felton turned to garlic for help. Teammate Ron Davis kept a collection of garlic cloves hanging on a rope in his locker room cubicle to ward off negative spirits. Davis rubbed the garlic on Felton's shoulders. Nobody knew if the negative spirits stayed away—but most definitely the victories did.

"Well, records are made to be broken," philosophized Twins manager Billy Gardner. He said he continued to use Felton because the Twins, who were in last place at the time, had no one better in the bullpen. But at least the rest of the pitching corps manged to win a game now and then.

If it wasn't Felton's pitching mistakes it was his fielding errors that cost him victories. In his fifteenth loss, for example, Felton had thrown a no-hitter for five innings against Seattle. But things fell apart for him and the Twins in the sixth. After giving up two singles, Felton fielded a double play ball and threw wildly to second base. Two batters later, Felton was replaced, trailing 2–1. The Mariners went on to win 10–2.

Manager Billy Gardner did everything he could to give Felton a shot at victory as the 1982 season neared its end. Gardner used Felton to relieve starter Brad Havens in the fourth inning with the Twins leading the Kansas City Royals 7–4. Havens could not win the game because a starter must go five innings to be credited with a victory. That meant Felton could have captured his first win ever with a few decent innings of relief work. He even had a three-run cushion.

But Felton couldn't make it through two innings. He departed in the sixth with a 7–6 lead, leaving two runners on base. Both scored against reliever Ron Davis (the same guy who rubbed garlic on Felton's shoulders) as the Royals crushed the Twins 18–7. It was Felton's sixteenth and final loss of his career. The Twins finally "waived" him goodbye.

Czar Wars

The Dumbest Rulings by the Commissioner's Office

The commissioners are the great wise men of baseball, the pure of heart who must rule on issues that are in the best interest of the game. They are not afraid to make decisions. It's just that they don't always know what decisions to make. When they do decide, unfortunately, it's often wrong. For "The Dumbest Rulings by the Commissioner's Office," The Baseball Hall of SHAME inducts the following:

Judge Kenesaw Mountain Landis
1920

Landis was the game's first and most powerful commissioner. The lords of baseball spent twenty-four years kicking themselves for putting him in office rather than someone they could manipulate more easily.

The image of Landis is that of a benevolent dictator, stern but fair, impartial and incorruptible, the man who saved baseball. But Landis had a shameful side the public rarely saw. During his reign, "Equal justice under the law," came to mean "Unequal justice under Landis."

Landis came to power as a result of the so-called Black Sox Scandal of 1919. His first action was to severely punish those Chicago White Sox players who had been accused of throwing the World Series.

As a federal judge, Landis had sworn to preserve the American ideal of innocent until proven guilty. But as commissioner, he totally ignored that cherished concept in dealing with the Chicago players. A jury found them not guilty of conspiracy charges but Landis was not going to be intimidated by the law.

He ordered that they be banned from baseball forever. The lifetime bans meant they couldn't even buy a ticket to a professional game! The records of each player were stricken from the books, including the .356 lifetime batting average of Shoeless Joe Jackson.

He warned that any player who so much as heard of a plot to fix games and didn't report it would get the same thing.

But his statements oozed of hypocrisy. The sanctimonious commissioner did nothing to others with "guilty knowledge" of the conspiracy to fix the Series. Included were people like Rube Benton, a pitcher for the Giants who, according to trial testimony, picked up a quick $3,200 by betting on his former teammates, the underdog Cincinnati Reds. A few years later, Benton was trying to come back from the minors. The presidents of both leagues said they wouldn't allow him to play. But Landis interfered and Benton rejoined the Reds.

Another smelly figure in the whole affair who escaped untouched by Landis' wrath was Hal Chase, whose career was one accusation after another of involvement in fixed games. He was mentioned as a major link between the gamblers and the players in the Black Sox Scandal.

Landis' ability to talk out of both sides of his mouth surfaced again in 1926. Within a month of each other Ty Cobb of the Tigers and Tris Speaker of the Indians, both player-managers, mysteriously resigned. Later, Landis announced that both had decided to quit rather than face charges by former pitcher Dutch Leonard that they had bet on a fixed game, also in 1919. However, when Landis made known the reason for their retirements both asked to be reinstated to confront the charges. While he was studying the evidence against the two stars, yet a third betting scandal emerged. Swede Risberg, one of the Black Sox players claimed that in 1917 the Tigers had thrown a four-game series to the White Sox and about 50 players were involved. Some members of both teams even admitted that money had changed hands.

But Landis chose to ignore all charges. Instead, he declared that from then on, there would be a statute of limitations on past corruption. Nothing was done to any of the players involved.

Cobb and Speaker returned to the game and eventual baseball sainthood. The Black Sox remained damned.

A.B. "Happy" Chandler
1947

No one really wanted Happy Chandler as a successor to Kenesaw Mountain Landis, but Yankee owner Larry MacPhail orchestrated his appointment.

A few years later, Chandler returned the favor with his despicable suspension of Brooklyn Dodgers manager Leo Durocher.

MacPhail and Durocher had been bad mouthing each other ever since the early 1940s when Larry ruled the Dodgers and Leo was his manager. The feud boiled over during spring training in Havana in 1947. Durocher had already been warned by Chandler to cut out his associations with actor George Raft and other "unsavory" characters connected with gambling.

However, a couple of high rollers with casino connections in Havana showed up with MacPhail behind the Yankee dugout during exhibition games. Durocher complained to Chandler about the double standard. Also, an article highly critical of MacPhail and ghost-written by Harold Parrott, the Dodgers traveling secretary, appeared in a Brooklyn newspaper under Leo's byline.

Now the bitterness was out in the open and MacPhail went to his buddy in the commissioner's office and filed a bill of particulars charging Leo with "conduct detrimental to baseball." Chandler held two hearings on the matter. Both were closed to the press and public. He also ordered all the participants to keep their mouths shut about what went on.

Just before the season opened, Chandler announced his decision. Durocher was suspended for one year and Parrott was fined $500 for writing the article that made MacPhail look bad. MacPhail got off scot-free and nobody knew why. Chandler refused to discuss his ruling and his tight lid of secrecy applied to the others in the case. The only explanation ever offered for Leo's suspension was "an accumulation of unpleasant incidents" which Durocher was allegedly involved in "which the Commissioner construes as detrimental to baseball."

Chandler's handling of the situation was detrimental to baseball. The owners booted him out of office in 1951.

Ford Frick*

1961

Put a big fat asterisk beside Frick's name in the history book. It matches the one he ordered placed beside Roger Maris' name in the record books when the slugger broke Babe Ruth's home run mark in 1961.

Frick had a selfish reason for branding an asterisk on Maris' 61 homers. The commissioner had been a long-time Ruth lover from the days when he had covered the Yankees as a sportswriter. He had even ghost-written articles under Ruth's name during that period when the press conspired to cover up the Babe's indiscretions. Frick had built a career tagging along on

Ruth's coattails, so he had a personal reason to rub a little of the shine off Maris' accomplishment.

When both Maris and Mickey Mantle looked like they had a shot at the record, Frick announced in the middle of the 1961 season that to "officially" break the record they would have to hit 61 homers within 154 games. As Maris pointed out later, which 154? The first 154 games? The last? The middle?

When Frick came up with the nutty asterisk idea, Maris didn't say much. But the fans did. They came to the park with posters denouncing the decision. "Frick—Up Your Asterisk!" was one of the milder ones.

On Oct. 1, 1961, Maris parked a 2–0 fastball from Red Sox pitcher Tracy Stallard in the right field seats at Yankee Stadium. It was Number 61 and the hated asterisk became part of baseball history. It's gone from the record book now, but its shadow remains in the dual classification of 154 and 162 games for determining records.

Bowie Kuhn

1981

Bowie Kuhn, supposedly the most powerful man in baseball at the time, sat helplessly during an unprecedented 59-day players' strike that threatened to destroy not only baseball's popularity but its integrity as well.

He blundered badly when he announced publicly that he would do everything in his power to settle the strike. And then he did nothing while the owners, despite their strike insurance, lost money. And greedy bosses don't cotton to any hired help who costs them money.

Although he finally got involved and helped end the mid-season strike, Kuhn then cheated the players and fans out of a meaningful pennant race. He force-fed everyone a split season with an insane playoff system.

Seven weeks of the baseball year were lost to the strike and since the games couldn't possibly be made up, Kuhn devised a convoluted plan. He divided the season in two parts. The division leaders at the time of the strike would be matched against the leaders with the best records following the strike. The mini-series would determine each divisional champion.

As a result of Kuhn's mind-boggling scheme, some of the year's best teams didn't make the playoffs. The Cincinnati Reds had the best overall record in baseball that year with a 66–42 mark yet didn't qualify for postseason play. The Kansas City Royals, who otherwise would have finished fourth in the A.L. West, earned a mini-series date with Oakland.

Somehow, baseball managed to stumble through the season—no thanks to Bowie Kuhn.

Cinema Sins

The Worst Baseball Movies

There are some things that just naturally don't belong together. Cats and dogs. Yankees and Dodgers. Movies and baseball. Hollywood flicks have degraded baseball and been an embarrassment to watch. The mystery is why they were ever made in the first place. The wonder is that people paid to see them. The miracle is that baseball survived despite them. For "The Worst Baseball Movies," The Baseball Hall of SHAME inducts the following:

The Babe Ruth Story
1948

This was the worst baseball movie ever made. It was a staggering box-office flop and deserved the scathing reviews it received.

Casting William Bendix to portray Babe Ruth made about as much sense as sending in the bat boy to pinch hit for Dale Murphy. About the only thing Bendix and Ruth had in common was the size of their bellies.

Bendix wore a fake putty nose that wiggled around when he acted (the word "acted" is used here very loosely). He portrayed the Babe as an expressionless Neanderthal.

Worse yet, Bendix swung the bat like Ma Kettle shooing the goats out of the garden with a broom. Being right-handed, Bendix had to learn to bat and throw left-handed. He learned, but he wasn't very good at it. In

fact, during the filming of a scene in which he was to hit three fly balls, Bendix could only hit two in thirty minutes of futile takes.

In defense of Bendix, he was saddled with one of the worst scripts ever penned in Hollywood. The movie played fast and loose with the truth and relied on maudlin clichés and downright lies.

Would anyone believe Babe Ruth sitting down in a bar and ordering a glass of milk? Bendix does in the movie—and audiences everywhere gagged at the unbelievable sight.

In another scene written out of whole cloth, a mangy dog wanders out onto the playing field during spring training and gets hit by a line drive off Ruth's bat. The Babe picks up the mutt and rushes him to a veterinarian for emergency surgery only to have Yankee manager Miller Huggins fine him $500 for being absent without permission.

If the movie had been true, then Ruth definitely missed his calling. He should have been a faith healer. In one scene, he tosses off a casual "Hi ya, kid," to a crippled little boy. With the music swelling, the kid is so inspired by his hero's words that he rises from his seat and walks.

This movie deserves three strikes.

Slide, Kelly, Slide

1927

Some real big league ball players participated in this criminal act—Bob Meusel, Tony Lazzeri, and Mike Donlin. And the Yankees compounded the felony by allowing Yankee Stadium and their spring training camp in Florida to be used as settings.

Even by Hollywood's outlandish standards, *Slide, Kelly, Slide*, was a piece of mawkish trash, starring William Haines as Kelly and Harry Carey as an aging catcher.

In the film, Kelly is a hotshot New York Yankees pitcher with bush league brains. After pitching a no-hitter, Kelly turns to bootleg booze and gets hooked by demon rum. All washed up, he confesses to the old catcher, whose daughter dumps the pitcher because he's spending his free time in the gutter. Even the team mascot, a little boy named Mickey, who once idolized Kelly, can't stand the bum.

Here, the script crosses the threshold of absurdity. It's the day of the dramatic seventh game of the World Series against the St. Louis Cardinals. Convinced the team can't win without Kelly, the old catcher pleads with the Yankees to give Kelly one more chance. The manager agrees.

Mickey joyfully jumps on his bike and peddles off to tell Kelly the good news but a fire truck runs over the boy. The doctors decide the only thing that will restore Mickey's will to live is to watch the decisive game from the box seats.

There, all bandaged up, Mickey watches Kelly twirl a masterful game. But the score is tied 1–1 in the last of the ninth inning when who should come to bat but Kelly. He looks over at the seats and sees little Mickey down on his knees, praying for a hit.

Naturally, Kelly hits a home run and the movie ends with him marrying the catcher's daughter while Mickey dances around like any fool who had been hit by a fire truck would.

Safe at Home

1962

The only way fans may ever see this sorry excuse for a movie is if some hard-up TV station has air time to fill between 3 A.M. and 4:30 A.M.

That's assuming that Yankee sluggers Roger Maris and Mickey Mantle, who starred in this turkey, didn't buy up and destroy all copies of the crummy flick.

The dippy B-picture story line is about a 10-year-old Little Leaguer who lies to his friends about his close, personal friendship with the New

York Yankees. When he's forced to back up his boast, the dumb kid runs away from home and heads for the Yankees' spring training camp in Fort Lauderdale, Florida. After sneaking into the clubhouse, the boy meets his heroes, Mantle and Maris, and begs them to attend the Little League banquet so he can prove to his buddies back home that the M & M boys are his pals.

About the only thing the two sluggers do well in the movie is belt a few fast balls out of the park. However, when it comes to acting, Mantle and Maris go down swinging.

Their performance was as awkward as the dialogue they were forced to read. In front of the camera, their acting closely resembled their bats— very wooden. They look about as comfortable as rookies in their first game. Too bad they weren't benched.

No doubt this movie was made for one reason—to exploit the popularity of Maris and Mantle, who in the previous season walloped 61 and 54 homers respectively.

It's a shame such big leaguers allowed themselves to star in such a minor league production. Judging from the box office receipts, movie-goers called *Safe at Home* "out" at the theater.

The Fall Follies

The Most Atrocious World Series Performances

The World Series isn't always all that it's cracked up to be. Naturally, the lords of baseball want everyone to believe that the October extravaganza showcases the leagues' two best teams with dazzling fielding, thrilling base running, dynamite hitting and awesome pitching. In truth the Fall Classic is often the Classic Fall from grace to disgrace for so-called champions. For "The Most Atrocious World Series Performances," The Baseball Hall of SHAME inducts the following:

Los Angeles Dodgers
1966

It was as if the Dodgers bat rack carried a sign that read "Do Not Disturb." During the Series against the Baltimore Orioles, the Los Angeles hitters—a contradiction in terms—could have taken batting practice in a china shop and not broken a single plate.

In the worst hitting performance in Series history, the puny Dodgers could only muster an anemic .142 batting average. Lou Johnson "led" all Dodger regulars with a meager .267 average.

The Dodgers further shamed themselves by establishing or tying new lows in the Series record book: most times consecutively shut out, three; most consecutive scoreless innings, 33; fewest total bases, 23; and fewest runs scored—just two!

Not to be out-embarrassed, Dodger centerfielder Willie Davis set his own black mark. It happened in the fifth inning of the second game. He moved in on a routine pop fly by Paul Blair, lost it in the sun and dropped it for an error. Andy Etchebarren came up and lofted another soft fly to center. Incredibly, Davis did a repeat performance of his blunder and dropped this ball too for another error. Now totally mortified, Davis grabbed the ball and threw wildly past third. Three miscues in one inning by one player! A new Series record!

Perhaps it was best that the Dodgers lost the Series in a four-game sweep. They were quickly put out of their misery.

St. Louis Browns (A.A.) vs. Chicago White Stockings (N.L.)

1885

It was the fielding—or more aptly the lack of it—that vaulted this Series into the annals of fall foolishness. Never in baseball history have two teams displayed such amazing incompetence, making more errors than hits.

The blundering players muffed easy grounders, dropped routine pop flies and threw wildly in every single Series game to rack up an incredible 102 errors—six more than the number of hits they collected. But who needed hits with such phenomenally inept fielding?

Both teams worked hard at beating themselves. The relentless error production continued throughout the Series—15 in the first game, 9 the next, then 16, 10, 8 and 17.

But the "Boys of Bummer" saved the worst for last. Floundering on the field in the final game, St. Louis booted the ball ten times only to be topped by 17 Chicago errors.

The fourth inning was a classic for Chicago's clod squad. With a flair for botchery seldom seen on the baseball diamond, Cap Anson let two feeble grounders trickle through his legs, left fielder Abner Dalrymple unleashed a wild throw two stories over the catcher's head, shortstop Ned Williamson fired a strike into the seats and catcher Frank "Silver" Flint let two pitched strikes slip through his fingers for passed balls. As a testament to the caliber of fielding, the record book shows that 13 of the 17 total runs scored in the game were unearned.

Although this fielding alone was worthy of dishonor, the 1885 Series disgraced itself in other ways as well.

The White Stockings didn't earn their first victory. It was given to them. In the sixth inning of the second game with Chicago leading 5–4, St. Louis player-manager Charlie Comiskey was so enraged by a bad call by umpire Dan Sullivan that he yanked his team off the field in protest. Sullivan countered by declaring the game a forfeit. But St. Louis won a moral victory when Sullivan was relieved of his umpiring duties for the rest of the Series because of his poor officiating.

So where did all this on-the-field incompetence lead? Nowhere. The Series ended in a tie. And in controversy. Since each team had won three and tied once (the first game was called on account of darkness with the score knotted at 5–5), Chicago's Cap Anson declared his White Stockings co-champions. But the Browns claimed the championship for themselves, insisting that the forfeited second game should not count. At least one fact remains undisputed. The Series was so bad it easily secured its rightful place in The Baseball Hall of SHAME.

1st Game, at Chicago, Oct. 14					R	H	E
St. Louis (AA)	010	400	00	—	5	7	4
Chicago (NL)	000	100	04	—	5	6	11

(called, end of 8th: darkness)
Pitchers—Caruthers vs. Clarkson. Homer—Pfeffer (Chi.). Attendance—3,000.

2nd Game, at St. Louis, Oct. 15						
Chicago (NL)	110	003	—	5	6	5
St. Louis (AA)	300	10x	—	4	2	4

(Game forfeited to Chicago, 9-0)
Pitchers—McCormick vs Foutz. Attendance—2,000.

3rd Game, at St. Louis, Oct. 16							
Chicago (NL)	111	000	001	—	4	8	12
St. Louis (AA)	500	002	00x	—	7	8	4

Pitchers—Clarkson vs. Caruthers. Att.—3,000

4th Game, at St. Louis, Oct. 17							
Chicago (NL)	000	020	000	—	2	8	3
St. Louis (AA)	001	000	02x	—	3	6	7

Pitchers—McCormick vs. Foutz. Homer—Dalrymple (Chi.). Attendance—3,000.

5th Game, at Pittsburgh, Oct. 22							
Chicago (NL)	400	110	3	—	9	7	1
St. Louis (AA)	010	000	1	—	2	4	7

(called, end of 7th: darkness)
Pitchers—Clarkson vs. Foutz. Attendance—500.

6th Game, at Cincinnati, Oct. 23							
Chicago (NL)	200	111	040	—	9	11	10
St. Louis (AA)	002	000	000	—	2	2	7

Pitchers—McCormick vs. Caruthers. Attendance—1,500.

7th Game, at Cincinnati, Oct. 24							
Chicago (NL)	200	020	00	—	4	9	17
St. Louis (AA)	004	621	0x	—	13	12	10

(called in 8th: darkness)
Pitchers—McCormick vs. Foutz. Attendance—1,200.

Fred Snodgrass
OUTFIELDER

Chief Meyers
CATCHER

Christy Mathewson
PITCHER

Fred Merkle
FIRST BASEMAN

NEW YORK, N.L. · OCT. 16, 1912

People say that Fred Snodgrass lost the Series for the Giants. But blame is a lot like fertilizer. You must spread it around where it belongs. No team ever handed a Series championship to its opponents the way these Giants did.

The Giants and the Red Sox had each won three games. Since one other game had ended in a 6–6 tie, the stage was set for an unusual eighth game in Fenway Park. In the final game, the Giants scored a run in the tenth and took a 2–1 lead.

In the Boston half of the tenth, pinch hitter Clyde Engle hit an ordinary fly ball to center, the territory of the sure-handed Fred Snodgrass. But the unbelievable happened. The ball thudded into Snodgrass' glove and then plopped to the ground. Engle raced to second. The outfielder tried to atone for his grave mistake with a sensational catch on the next ball but the Giants were still shaken up. The team began to fall apart at the seams.

The famous control of Giant pitcher Christy Mathewson suddenly vanished and he walked weak-hitting Steve Yerkes. That brought up the always dangerous Tris Speaker. On the first pitch, Speaker popped up a lazy foul between first and home. Any one of three players could have caught it with their eyes closed. Mathewson moved over from the mound, catcher Chief Meyers broke from the plate and first baseman Fred Merkle trotted down the baseline. What followed was a scene straight out of a Three Stooges flick. Mathewson called for Meyers to take it. But Meyers thought Merkle had it. Merkle thought Meyers *and* Mathewson had it. Nobody had it. All three stood there and watched the ball fall to the ground at their feet. And with that blunder, the outcome was inevitable— and everybody in Fenway Park knew it.

Given a new lease on life, Speaker singled to right to drive in Engle with the tying run. Duffy Lewis was intentionally passed to load the bases. Larry Gardner then hit a sacrifice fly to score Yerkes with the winning run for the world championship.

After such an amazing collapse, Mathewson, Meyers, Merkle and Snodgrass should have gone into another line of work—the demolition business.

Cincinnati Reds

1919

Everybody knows that the 1919 World Series was tainted by the infamous Black Sox Scandal when several Chicago players were accused of taking payoffs to throw the Series.

But the Reds' performance was shameful as well. They almost lost to a team that was doing everything in its power to hand them victory.

Even though the White Sox fix was on, it looked more like the Reds who were the ones taking the dive in the best of nine series. After all, they committed just as many errors as the White Sox, 12.

For instance, in the second inning of the third game, Cincinnati pitcher Ray Fisher fielded a sacrifice bunt and flung the ball over second base into center field. That put runners at second and third. A single brought them home. Chicago was given another run by the Reds and reluctantly won, 3–0.

The White Sox tried to give the Reds the sixth game but Cincy refused to take it. Doing everything but pick up the Reds and carry them around the bases, the White Sox committed three errors to give Cincinnati a 4–0 lead. But the Reds successfully fought off victory with an abominable display of baseball at its worst.

Chicago batter Buck Weaver looped a pop fly to short left field that should have been an easy catch for either left fielder Pat Duncan or shortstop Larry Kopf. Instead, they stood around and watched to see how high the ball would bounce when it hit the ground. Weaver ran at less than full speed but the Reds still couldn't throw him out. The goof paved the way for a 5–4 Chicago victory.

The Reds bats went silent in the seventh game so the White Sox won again, 4–1. Faced with an eighth game, there was real desperation in the Chicago clubhouse that they might actually win the Series after all. But the Reds finally came through, winning 10–5 after White Sox hurler Claude Williams grooved enough pitches to get bombed in the first inning.

The better team probably didn't win the Series. The better loser lost it.

Hack Wilson

OUTFIELDER · CHICAGO, N.L. · Oct. 12, 1929

When the 1929 World Series had faded into painful memory, Chicagoans were mournfully singing "The Wrigley Field Blues." It was sung slowly and with great feeling to the tune of "My Old Kentucky Home."

The first stanza went: "Oh! The sun shone bright in our great Hack

Wilson's eyes ..." And it concluded: "Weep no more, dear Cub fan/Oh, weep no more today/ For we'll sing one song for the game and fighting Cubs/ For the record-whiffing Cubs far away."

The Chicago fans had a right to vent their bitterness not only over the Cubs' World Series loss to Philadelphia but also over Hack Wilson and his absentmindedness. He opened the way for an astonishing come-from-behind victory by the A's which became the turning point of the Series.

Going into the seventh inning at Shibe Park, Cubs ace Charlie Root was throwing a three-hitter, smugly anticipating victory with what looked like an insurmountable 8–0 lead. A win by the Cubs would even the Series at two games apiece.

The A's Al Simmons opened the inning with a home run and Jimmy Foxx singled, but there was no cause for alarm. Next, Bing Miller lofted a short fly to center. Wilson ran in and reached to flip down his sunglasses. Everybody wore sunglasses in the outfield at Shibe because of the glare. Everybody, that is, except Hack. He had accidently left his back in the dugout. Without the sunglasses, Hack was blinded by the sun and dropped Miller's ball.

Incredibly, before the next batter stepped up, Hack did not call time to fetch his sunglasses. His failure to do so spelled doom for him and his Cubs.

The A's kept the rally alive and had cut the lead to 8–4 with two runners on when Mule Haas smashed a long fly ball toward Hack. Again, Hack was blinded by the sun and stood helplessly as the ball sailed over his head for a three-run, inside-the-park homer. The Cubs collapsed as the A's tallied 10 runs in the inning for a Series record.

Devastated by the loss, the Cubs played dead the next day as the A's won the world championship.

Sighed Cub manager Joe McCarthy: "Sometimes I think nine trained monkeys could do better in a Series than the apes we pay salaries."

Sore Losers

The Most Outrageous Reactions to a Loss

Accepting defeat gracefully is the sign of a wimp. Real losers don't take losing lying down. They fling bats, helmets, and towels out of the dugout. They rant and rave, blaming everybody but themselves. However, these acts are nothing more than hackneyed baseball theatrics. A true shameful performance calls for histrionics and showmanship to turn mere losing into a classic melodramatic spectacle. For "The Most Outrageous Reactions to a Loss," The Baseball Hall of SHAME inducts the following:

Mark Lemongello

PITCHER · HOUSTON, N.L.; TORONTO, A.L. · 1976–79

Lemongello put on such a display of havoc whenever he lost a game that his own teammates scurried to the clubhouse just to watch the show. He ravaged everything in sight, including hair dryers, mirrors, lockers—even his own body.

Once in a fit of rage, he bit his shoulder until it bled. Another time he pounded on his pitching hand with his other fist and almost broke it. He also kicked a cigarette machine with such force that he was cut by the flying glass.

After another horribly pitched game, Mark roared into the clubhouse in a fury and dove headlong onto a buffet table laden with food. Recalled a former teammate who had to find somewhere else to eat: "He just lay there covered with mustard and butter for half an hour."

For his teammates—as long as they stayed clear of the angry pitcher—Lemongello's performances made losing almost worthwhile.

Moe Drabowsky

PITCHER · CHICAGO-MILWAUKEE-CINCINNATI-ST. LOUIS, N.L.
BALTIMORE-KANSAS CITY-CHICAGO, A.L. · 1956–72

Some losers throw chairs. Drabowsky threw rooms.

One of his worst tantrums cost him a bundle after a particularly tough loss on the road. Drabowsky stormed back to the team's hotel and went ten rounds with his room. The room lost.

He singlehandedly smashed walls, tables, chairs, lights, windows, even a sink. He finished it off by knocking down the door.

When he was done with his redecorating, Drabowsky was presented with a bill for $5,600 in damages.

Fred Hutchinson

MANAGER · DETROIT, A.L. · ST. LOUIS-CINCINNATI, N.L.
1952–54, 1956–58, 1963–64

Next to hanging curves, Hutch hated losing more than anything in the world. His red-hot temper could scare his players spitless.

Hutch's wrath once shook the rafters at County Stadium in Milwaukee when Joe Nuxhall was pitching against the Braves.

The Reds were leading by two runs with two out and nobody on in the bottom of the ninth. Hutch was smiling happily over the apparent victory, but a single, an error and a hanging curve that turned into a three-run homer wiped the smile right off his face.

Snorting fire, the manager grabbed a bat and glowered at Nuxhall, who was too terrified to come off the mound. The infuriated Hutchinson then stormed down the runway, smashing the lights as he went. In the clubhouse, he thundered: "Where is that damned lefthander?" Nuxhall knew better than to show his face in the clubhouse in the middle of that rampage. Instead, the trembling pitcher ran out to the street—in full uniform—hailed a cab, headed straight for the safety of his hotel room and locked himself in!

AP/Wide World Photo

After another loss, Hutch sat in the dugout alone steaming like an overheated teakettle while his players scurried for the showers. He fumed a few minutes, then picked up the dugout phone and called the clubhouse attendant. "If any of those idiots are still there," he growled, "tell them to get out because I'm coming in!" The attendant later remembered the scene. "When that phone rang," he said, "there were about a dozen or so half-dressed players still hanging around. When Hutch walked in three minutes later there was nobody there but me."

Moses "Lefty" Grove

PITCHER · PHILADELPHIA-BOSTON, A.L. · 1925–41

It took courage to be on the same team with Grove when he lost. Woe be to anyone who dropped a fly or flubbed a grounder while he was pitching. And if the error cost him the game, the rack would have been more enjoyable than facing Grove in the clubhouse.

In a game against the miserable St. Louis Browns in 1931, teammate Jim Moore misjudged a ninth-inning fly ball, costing Grove not only a shutout but a victory as the Browns won 1–0.

Grove stormed off the mound with Jim Moore in his eye and murder on his mind. He exploded into the clubhouse like a shot from a cannon while Moore desperately searched for a place to hide. Grove screamed at everyone in sight, throwing gloves, shoes, and most everything that wasn't bolted down. He tore up the benches and ripped lockers off the wall. All the while, Moore cowered in the showers in mortal fear of his life.

After wrecking the place, Grove caught the train home and spent several days sulking and pouting behind closed doors, refusing to show up at the ballpark. When he finally did appear, Grove wouldn't even talk to his teammates, which was fine with them. By then, he didn't have any friends left to talk to anyway.

Wes Ferrell

PITCHER · CLEVELAND-BOSTON-WASHINGTON-NEW YORK, A.L.
1927–41

Now here was a guy who hated to lose. Often when the right hander was pulled out of a game, he started throwing punches—at himself. Rampaging through the clubhouse, Ferrell would pound himself so hard on the jaw that he would almost knock himself out.

After especially tough losses, he paid dearly for his anger. A lover of fancy watches, Ferrell had the unfortunate and expensive habit of grabbing his latest timepiece, hurling it to the floor and stomping on it after a bad showing on the mound. Because he suffered a fair amount of bitter defeats, Ferrell made many trips to the watchmaker.

Warped Records

The Titles Most Tarnished by Chicanery

In no other game are records and titles so revered. We crown the home-run king and the batting champ. We honor the pitchers with the most wins and lowest ERA. Their records stand as benchmarks for the best baseball has to offer. Yet the simple numbers fail to reveal untold stories of the worst baseball has to offer— attempted bribery, complicity, shadiness, and guile. For "The Titles Most Tarnished by Chicanery," The Baseball Hall of SHAME inducts the following:

Ty Cobb's Batting Title

1910

There were shady shenanigans on both sides of this classic duel for the batting crown. Pitted against one another were Nap Lajoie, one of baseball's best loved players, and Ty Cobb, one of the game's most hated men. To everyone in the American League, it was a clear-cut case of Good versus Evil.

Lajoie, second baseman for the Cleveland Indians, and Cobb, outfielder for the Detroit Tigers, had battled neck and neck all season for the batting title. Coming down to the final day of the season, Cobb held a comfortable .009-point lead over Lajoie.

Showing his true colors, the Georgia Peach took the chickenhearted way out. He benched himself rather than risk a bad day at the plate and thus lose a few points that could cost him the title.

Meanwhile, Cleveland was in St. Louis for a double-header. Since neither team was in contention and everyone was pulling for Lajoie to win the batting title, Browns manager Jack O'Connor decided to help. He started rookie Red Corriden at third base with orders to play back on the grass when Lajoie batted. "He's liable to take your head off with a line drive," O'Connor advised with a wink.

The first time up, Lajoie did indeed slash a triple. But on his second trip to the plate, he couldn't help but notice that Corriden was playing third base from somewhere in left field. Lajoie dropped a bunt down the third base line and easily beat it out. The next two times up, he also bunted safely toward a vacant third base and went four-for-four in the first game.

With his batting average now soaring, Lajoie repeated the performance in game two while Corriden continued to hold his position in short left to avoid having his head taken off by one of Lajoie's vicious bunts.

On his last appearance of the day, Lajoie changed tactics and hit a sharp grounder to Bobby Wallace at short. Wallace muffed the play and was charged with an error. This meant that Lajoie officially had a hitless at-bat. Browns coach Harry Howell rushed to the official scorer, a woman, and begged her to change the error to a clean hit. He even offered to buy her a new wardrobe, but she refused the bribe and the error stood.

The scheme to help Lajoie failed. In the end, Cobb edged him out by a miniscule .0007 of a point, .3848 to .3841, much to the disappointment of Lajoie's friends.

The unhappiest of all were Browns manager Jack O'Connor and his coach Harry Howell. They were kicked out of baseball permanently for trying to give the batting title to Lajoie.

Chuck Klein's Home Run Title

1929

The home-run crown that Chuck Klein wore came courtesy of his unsporting Phillies teammates.

Klein and New York Giants outfielder Mel Ott each led the league with 42 homers on the last day of the season. The Giants were in the Baker Bowl for a double-header, a backdrop to one of those rare confrontations between two title-seekers. But the despicable actions of the Phillies pitchers cheated Mel Ott out of a shot at the crown.

In the first game, Klein powered a home run to put him one ahead of Ott who was held to a single. In the second game, the Phillies pitchers guaranteed that Klein would win the title. They deliberately walked Ott in the first, fourth, sixth, eighth and ninth innings. And to prove what cowards they were, one of those walks came with the bases loaded!

Mickey Vernon's Batting Title

1953

The 1953 Washington Senators helped rob Cleveland Indian Al Rosen of the batting title and, thus, the coveted Triple Crown. Rosen, who led the league in homers and RBIs, was virtually tied for the lead in batting average with Senators first baseman Mickey Vernon.

On the final day of the season, the Indians faced the Tigers who tried to be helpful to Rosen by playing their infield back whenever he batted so he had all the room he needed to bunt. But showing his class (or his stupidity, depending on your point of view) Rosen wanted no favors and instead hit away, rapping two singles and a double in five at-bats.

Meanwhile, Vernon picked up two hits in four at-bats against the Athletics when word came from his teammates who were monitoring the Cleveland-Detroit game that Rosen was finished for the day. Vernon would win the title outright if he didn't have to bat again.

He was to be the fourth batter up in the last inning so his teammates made sure he wouldn't face another at-bat. With one out, Mickey Grasso doubled but was conveniently picked off when he casually stepped off the bag. Kite Thomas singled but he leisurely strolled to second "trying" to stretch the hit into a double and was thrown out for the third out.

Mickey Vernon was left standing near the dugout with a big grin on his face, a bat in his hand and the batting crown on his head—a crown he won by only .0011 points.

Don Drysdale's Consecutive
Shutout Innings Record

1968

The Los Angeles Dodgers fireballer should be a big man and offer to share his record of 58 consecutive shutout innings with umpire Harry Wendelstedt.

Drysdale was working on a string of 36 scoreless innings when the San Francisco Giants played the Dodgers in late May. Going into the eighth inning with a 3–0 lead, it looked like another sure shutout performance for Drysdale. But then he lost his control and loaded the bases with no outs on two walks and a single. The record looked in jeopardy.

The next batter, Giants catcher Dave Dietz, ran the count to 2–2 when a Drysdale fastball smacked Dietz on the elbow. This was not unusual since Drysdale hit more batters (154) than any other pitcher in major league history. But this HBP was a biggie. It meant the end of the scoreless streak. Or did it?

Dietz started toward first as the three runners advanced. But home plate umpire Wendelstedt, well aware of Big D's record, called Dietz back to the plate and made the runners return to their bases. Citing an obscure rule that few had ever seen enforced—let alone heard of—the ump told the incredulous Dietz, "You didn't try to get out of the way."

Drysdale had lucked out. He had been handed another chance, and he made the most of it. Forced to bat again, Dietz popped out. Drysdale then coaxed a force at home and another popup to keep the now-tainted streak alive.

Crud Duds

The Most Awful Uniforms Ever Worn

Ever since Charlie Finley broke the color barrier in 1963 and dressed his Athletics in green and gold, teams have been donning uniforms that look like something a peacock lost and didn't want to find. The Cleveland Indians once resembled blood clots. The San Diego Padres remind you of tacos with legs and the gold Pirate uniforms belong on a team in the losers' bracket of a girls' softball tournament. Believe it or not, players have been forced to wear even more ridiculous fashions. For "The Most Awful Uniforms Ever Worn," the Baseball Hall of SHAME inducts the following:

The National League

1882

The most outlandish uniforms ever seen on a diamond had a mercifully short shelf life much to the relief of the players who had to prance around like fugitives from the fashion pages.

The idea of this dreadful experiment was to identify players and positions by colors rather than numbers. White was the compulsory color for all pants, belts and ties. But the jerseys came in various combinations, depending on the position: pitcher, light blue; catcher, scarlet; first baseman, scarlet and white; second baseman, orange and black; third baseman, gray and white; shortstop, maroon; left fielder, white; center fielder, red and black; right fielder, gray; substitute, green and another substitute, brown.

Obviously, it was an idea whose time had not yet come. The players made sure of that. The season was hardly underway before they rebelled and color-coded jerseys were put on irrevocable waivers.

Brooklyn Dodgers

1916

Jealous of the handsome pinstripes first sported by the cross-town Yankees a year earlier, the Dodgers of Brooklyn—where nothing in baseball was ever done in moderation—took the design a step further. At the start of the 1916 season, they trotted out in their new duds—checkered uniforms. Thus, they proved to the world that there truly is no accounting for taste.

They looked as if they'd just crawled off the world's largest waffle iron—half baked. But even that wasn't enough for the Dodgers. They had to add yet another silly frill—an interlocking "NY" monogram that was copied from the badge given to New York police and firemen for bravery. That figures. It took a hero to wear those checks in public.

Chicago White Sox

1976

Somewhere medals of valor are waiting for all those White Sox who were brave enough to actually play a game in Bermuda shorts.

Owner Bill Veeck (who else?) dreamed up the bizarre outfits—navy blue shorts with white shirts and blue lettering—"to showcase our wares." The only thing showcased were a lot of knobby knees and red faces.

The first and only time the Sox appeared in their Little Lord Fauntleroy suits was the first game of a double-header with Kansas City on Aug. 8, 1976. Chicago won the game 5–2, mainly because the Royals collapsed in hysterics at the sight. "You guys are the sweetest team we've seen yet," cackled K.C. first baseman John Mayberry. Another player said Sox pitcher Clay Carroll looked like "a Pilgrim going out to shoot a wild turkey."

Between games of the double-header, the Sox abandoned their shorts and went back to wearing regular pants. Manager Paul Richards said they changed because it was getting too chilly for shorts. More likely it was Chicago's low humiliation tolerance. Besides, they didn't like wolf whistles.

Andy Messersmith

PITCHER · ATLANTA, N.L. · 1976

As a free agent who had just signed a multimillion-dollar contract with the Braves, Andy was more than willing to help owner Ted Turner with a shameful new wrinkle in self-promotion.

Turner thought it would be cute if Messersmith had a new nickname, so after careful thought, Turner came up with the clever name of "Channel" and had it sewn on the back of Messersmith's uniform. Then he decided to give the new pitcher number 17. Messersmith was all set. Whenever he walked out onto the field, the fans would look at the back of his uniform and realize that the Braves' new acquisition was "Channel 17."

By some strange coincidence, Channel 17 just happened to be owned by none other than Ted Turner whose super station telecasts Braves games across America. The ploy didn't last long. National League President Chub Feeney told Turner to call in his walking billboard forthwith.

Diamond Debacles

The Most Farcical Games Ever Misplayed

Baseball has endured many shameful blemishes that the purists would just as soon forget. The sport has been blighted by games which looked more like a Barnum & Bailey sideshow. Fans have been subjected to moments on the field that were too absurd for words. For "The Most Farcical Games Ever Misplayed," The Baseball Hall of SHAME inducts the following:

The Umpires' Strike
1979

A travesty is defined as a "grossly inferior imitation"—and the substitute arbiters who crossed the picket lines during the umpires' strike were most certainly grossly inferior.

They were so bad they created total chaos for the first 45 days of the 1979 season as they bumbled around the ballparks reversing decisions, tossing out players by the truckload and infuriating the fans to the point of a civil uprising. Most of the fake umps came out of the high school and college ranks. They never should have been allowed out of the sandlots.

One of the most disgraceful flaps caused by the strike occurred in Shea Stadium on April 24 in a game between the Mets and the Giants. For an incredible twenty-eight minutes, the four substitute umps puzzled over a disputed call, reversed their decision, changed their minds again and finally came up with an outrageous compromise that confused and angered both sides so much that each filed a protest.

With Mets Richie Hebner on first and Frank Taveras on third, batter Lee Mazzilli hit a long fly to outfielder Jack Clark who caught the ball and then dropped it while drawing back to make the throw. Taveras tagged and scored but Hebner, confused as to whether the ball had been caught for an out, was tagged between first and second base by infielder Bill Madlock.

High school umpire Phil Lospitalier signaled double play and was promptly besieged by Mets manager Joe Torre. After five minutes of arm-waving and fist-pounding, the umpires reversed themselves and put Hebner and Mazzilli on base. Then they were verbally assaulted by Giants manager Joe Altobelli. Finally, the umpires disappeared under the stands and emerged with a split decision: Mazzilli was out because Clark had caught the ball but Hebner was safe at first because he had been confused by the umpire.

That set the stage for the great debacle of May 9—the day the umps went wild. During that chaotic Wednesday, the muddleheads in blue threw out four managers, one coach and five players.

They let the game in Atlanta get completely out of control as four bench-clearing rhubarbs marred the Pirates 17–9 win over the Braves. Two of the brawls came in the ninth inning alone after four batters were hit by pitches. Both managers filed protests. "It was the worst excuse for umpiring I've ever seen," fumed Pirates catcher Ed Ott.

That same day in the Houston Astrodome, umpire Dave Pallone, a twenty-six-year-old minor league ump, cleared the St. Louis bench when the enraged Cardinals littered the field with bats and helmets in protest over his ruling that infielder Garry Templeton did not touch second on a force play.

In Fenway Park, California Angels manager Jim Fregosi was ordered to take a hike. He was furious over Don Baylor being called out for running outside the base path near third. Fregosi had good reason for seeing red. Baylor was called safe by the ump at third but was overruled by a minor league ump who made his call from behind second base.

Meanwhile, the Cleveland Indians' usually mild-mannered manager Jeff Torborg was given the heave-ho after flying into a rage over a balk call made by plate umpire Rick Reed who was working his first major league game. The balk was called in the ninth inning with the bases loaded and two outs. Fortunately, Cleveland managed to win anyway, 8–7.

The day's spectacle of incompetence did accomplish something. It brought enormous public pressure on baseball to settle the umpires' strike. The agreement that followed 10 days later preserved the game—and probably the lives of the scab arbiters.

Pittsburgh Pirates vs. Cincinnati Reds

OCT. 4, 1902

Cincinnati wanted the game cancelled but Pittsburgh didn't. Pittsburgh played to win but Cincinnati didn't. In the end, the fans lost.

The Pirates had raced away from the pack that year, finishing 27½ games in front of second place Brooklyn. The Reds, in fourth place, were 33½ games behind. On the last day of the season, the Pirates were one game away from a record at that time for the most victories in the league. They had won 102. They wanted victory number 103 in the worst way.

But it was a cold, drizzly day in Pittsburgh and the field was muddy. The Reds wanted the game called so they could go home for the season. Barney Dreyfuss, the Pirates owner, refused. He wanted that record and demanded that the umpires start the game. The umps meekly complied.

To get even, Cincinnati manager Joe Kelley told his players to make a sham of things. He played three left handers in the infield. He used three pitchers, none of whom had ever been on the mound before. One was outfielder Mike Donlin who had played in only 36 games. (He would have played more but he spent most of the season in jail for assaulting a woman on the street.)

Kelley sent rookie pitcher Harry "Rube" Vickers in to catch. Vickers, following orders, clowned his way through the game and set a record that still stands—six passed balls in a single game. Vickers made his performance even more pathetic by strolling along the way, pulling a hankie from his pocket and loudly blowing his nose.

The Cincinnati players brazenly smoked cigars on the field and added to the insult by blowing smoke in the Pirates' faces. Kelley himself strutted up to bat with a stogey in his mouth and ignored umpire Hank O'Day who told him to get rid of it.

The Pirates did win the laughingstock 11–2 to get the record, but Dreyfuss was incensed and threatened to have Kelley charged with unbecoming conduct on the field. Kelley replied that anyone who insisted on playing on a day like that ought to be arrested. Dreyfuss was so embarrassed by the farce—and in such danger of bodily harm from the indignant fans—that he refunded everyone's money.

The Pine Tar Bat Game

JULY 24, 1983

It took twenty-five days, one upheld protest, and two court decisions to complete this mockery of a baseball game.

Rich Gossage was pitching for the Yankees in the top of the ninth

inning with two outs when Kansas City Royals star George Brett smashed a two-run homer to give the Royals a 5–4 lead. Or so it seemed.

Yankee manager Billy Martin raced out of the dugout, rule book righteously in hand. Leading plate umpire Tim McClelland around by the nose, Martin smugly pointed out that the pine tar on Brett's bat exceeded the 18–inch limit. McClelland agreed and called Brett out for the third and final out of the game. The home run was disallowed. Therefore, the Yankees won 4–3. Or so it seemed.

Brett charged out of the dugout like an enraged bull. Umpiring crew chief Joe Brinkman held Brett around the neck to keep him from mauling McClelland. While Brett was screaming at the umps, the pine tar bat was passed from hand to hand and hustled out of sight into the Royals locker room. But stadium security guards retrieved the suspect lumber and later brought it to the umpire's room for safekeeping.

The Royals were incredulous that Brett had hit an apparent game-losing home run. "Broadway wouldn't buy that script," lamented K.C. manager Dick Howser who protested the game. "It wouldn't last past opening night, it's so unbelievable."

In the Yankee clubhouse, Martin couldn't contain his glee. He had known for two weeks that Brett's bat was technically illegal. But the cunning manager was waiting for the right time to protest—when Brett did something that hurt them. Said Billy with a smirk, "It turned out to be a lovely Sunday afternoon." Or so it seemed.

Four days later, American League President Lee MacPhail magnified the travesty even further by upholding the protest, declaring that although the pine tar was technically illegal, it didn't violate "the spirit of the rules." That meant the home run counted after all and the game would have to be continued with two out in the ninth inning and the Royals ahead 5–4.

Now it was the Yankees turn to howl. Snarled Yankee owner George Steinbrenner, "It sure tests our faith in our leadership." And in a typical veiled threat, Steinbrenner added, "I wouldn't want to be Lee MacPhail living in New York."

Billy Martin groused that he had never heard about the rules being "spiritual" and suggested that the rulebook "is only good for when you go deer hunting and run out of toilet paper.

"What Lee MacPhail has done is tell every kid in the country that they should go ahead and use illegal bats and cheat and they can get away with it."

The completion of the suspended game was set for August 18. The Yankees then crassly announced they would charge regular admission for the game and that brought an angry group of fans steaming into court. Two suits were filed protesting that the extra charge was illegal. An injunction prohibited the mini-game. Or so it seemed.

The fiasco made it all the way up to the Appellate Division of the New York Supreme Court where Justice Joseph P. Sullivan called a screeching halt to all the foolishness with perhaps the shortest ruling in legal history: Play ball!

The Yankees came sulking into the stadium still complaining. But few of the fans knew the team was there. The Yankees didn't bother announcing that management had reconsidered and fans with ticket stubs to the first game would be admitted without charge. Everyone else would have to pay $2.50 for the grandstand seats or $1 for the bleachers. Consequently, only about 1,200 fans showed up.

The completion required only nine minutes and 41 seconds. The Royals' Hal McRae struck out to end the top of the ninth. The Yankees went down in order in the last half of the inning.

A disgusted Don Baylor of the Yankees summed it up for baseball fans everywhere as he stalked off the field: "If I had wanted to watch a soap opera, I'd have stayed at home."

Detroit Tigers vs. Philadelphia Athletics

MAY 18, 1912

Ty Cobb gets the blame for the disgraceful events leading up to this sham at Shibe Park.

No longer content with mauling opponents on the field, Cobb charged into the stands in New York and beat up a heckler. The fact that the fan had no hands and could not defend himself mattered not the least to the Georgia Peach Pit. But it did matter to American League President Ban Johnson who slapped Cobb with a 10-day suspension for his despicable action.

To the amazement of everyone, the rest of the Tigers, who disliked Cobb as much as most everyone else in baseball, chose to support him. They refused to play until he was reinstated.

On May 18, three days later, the Tigers moved into Philadelphia to meet Connie Mack's Athletics. The papers were filled with strike talk and 15,000 fans came out expecting fireworks. Right up until game time, Detroit manager Hughie Jennings didn't know if he'd be able to field a professional team. He warned the players that by striking, the team faced a forfeit of the game, a $5,000 fine and possible loss of the franchise. But after finishing their warmups, the players swaggered off the field leaving only Jennings and coaches Joe Sugden and Jim McGuire to face the A's.

Jennings, though, was prepared. Earlier he had made the rounds in Philadelphia and recruited nine high school, college, and sandlot players eager to become Tigers for a day. He signed each to a $10 contract and hustled them into Detroit uniforms.

Predictably, the results were horrendous. Even with Mack charitably playing rookies and substitutes most of the game, the one-day wonders were still pounded 24–2. Sugden played first base, McGuire caught, and Jennings gave the pitching assignment to Al Travers who had once pitched for St. Joseph College.

The A's, as expected, shelled him. With no one to relieve him, Travers pitched the entire game. The A's—many so embarrassed they hit with one eye closed—whacked 26 hits off Travers who gave up a major league record 24 runs. Surprisingly, his teammates committed only eight errors before the slaughter ended.

Mack agreed to postpone the game the next day and the Tigers, meanwhile, voted to end their strike. As for Al Travers, he must have learned a profound lesson in humility during his one-day major league career. He joined the priesthood.

Washington Senators vs. Boston Red Sox

OCT. 4, 1913

The Boston Globe called it "the most farcical exposition of the national game that was ever staged." It sure was. This game belonged on a vaudeville stage.

Even though it was the last game of the season and its outcome would not affect the standings, the 8,000–plus fans had the right to see professional baseball. They didn't get it. From the opening pitch, the players, managers, and even the umpires disgraced themselves like burlesque comedians.

Eighteen different Senators played in the game and eight took a turn at pitching. At age forty-three, manager Clark Griffith himself went in to pitch one inning with his 44-year-old coach Jack Ryan as his catcher. Pitching ace Walter "The Big Train" Johnson was stationed in center field. Right fielder Germany Schaefer clowned around between first and second base rather than stay at his outfield position.

Boston infielders swapped positions with the outfielders and laughed at one another's antics. Veteran umpires Tom Connolly and Bill Dinneen joined the hijinks and even allowed four outs in one inning. Hurlers from both sides happily grooved pitches to give opposing buddies a chance to boost their batting averages.

In the ninth inning, with the Senators leading 10–3, Griffith looked to center field and told Walter Johnson to come to the mound. Johnson deliberately threw several fat pitches, giving up a single and double before Schaefer came in to pitch.

The Senators won the game 10–9, but when the records for the season were compiled, the league statistician ignored Johnson's minor pitching role in the farce game. Johnson was credited with an ERA of 1.09 for the year—a major league record for over 300 innings pitched in a single season.

But years later a diligent check of the game revealed that since Johnson had given up hits to two Red Sox players who eventually scored, both had to be counted as earned runs. Thus Johnson's official ERA for that year was adjusted upward to 1.14.

As a result, the magnificent record of "The Big Train" was derailed in 1968 when St. Louis Cardinals star pitcher Bob Gibson blazed his way to a stunning ERA of 1.12. If it wasn't for those two ridiculous hits in that mockery of a game, Walter Johnson would still own the ERA record.

The Death of the Toronto Seagull

AUG. 4, 1983

When the Yankees arrive in Toronto's Exhibition Stadium, a major portion of the local seagull population hightails it out of town until the coast is clear. Or at least until Dave Winfield retires.

The birds learned their lesson after one of their ilk deliberately got in front of a speeding baseball and then thoughtlessly dropped dead to put the blame on the Yankee outfielder. It was all part of a bird-brained scheme hatched by the winged cousins of the Blue Jays.

The nameless bird was part of the freeloading flock that routinely came gate-crashing to pick up a few handouts of spilled popcorn and hot dog buns.

The bird in question brazenly trespassed onto the field, thinking wrongly perhaps that foul territory was for the birds. The gull was obviously bent on suckering Winfield into trouble. It worked, for a while at least.

When Winfield threw a warmup ball off the field, the seagull stepped in the ball's path and was killed instantly. But the bird had accomplished its purpose of casting Winfield as a villain.

The crowd, seeing only a mound of feathers on the ground, accused Winfield of being a cold-blooded killer. They started peppering him with trash and booing him unmercifully as a batboy gently lay a towel over the late seagull and carried it away from the death scene.

After the game, Winfield was taken in tow by the local constabulary, cited for cruelty to animals and forced to post a $500 bond. But in the end, the bird's scheme went afoul. The charges were dropped.

Manager Billy Martin instantly saw right through the seagull conspiracy which tried to discredit his player. "Dave couldn't have hit the gull on purpose," Martin explained. "He hasn't hit the cutoff man all year!"

AP/Wide World Photo

Baseball's MBAs

Dishonorary Degrees for Managers of Blundering Actions

Those who can, do. Those who can't, teach. Those who can't do either, manage. And sometimes they don't do that very well. In fact, they'd have trouble managing a T-ball team. The lucky ones can mishandle the players, screw up the lineup, make the wrong moves, and still win because they have the horses. But if they have no talented players to hide behind, their mismanagement becomes glaring enough for all to see. For "Dishonorary Degrees for Managers of Blundering Actions," The Baseball Hall of SHAME inducts the following:

John J. McGraw
BALTIMORE, A.L. · NEW YORK, N.L. · 1902

The Little Napoleon managed—or more appropriately mismanaged—two different teams from two different leagues in the same season. And both teams ended up in the cellar.

McGraw first served as player-manager with the Orioles in the new American League. But he was in constant hot water with league president Ban Johnson over dirty tricks on the field. Early in the season, Johnson suspended McGraw indefinitely for his constant umpire-baiting. By then,

McGraw had led his Orioles to seventh place with a 28–34 mark.

This was also the period when the National League was fighting to squelch the upstart American League. In retaliation for his suspension, McGraw opened secret negotiations with owners in the rival league. A deal was cut and as part of the arrangements, McGraw moved to New York to take over the Giants' helm.

When he came on board, the Giants were floundering in eighth place. With McGraw now in charge, the team never budged from the cellar. Under his leadership, the Giants won 25 and lost 38 for a dead last finish with a horrendous overall record of 48–88, 53½ games out of first in the National League. With the losing start McGraw gave the Orioles in the American League, they also finished at the bottom with a 50–88 mark, 34 games behind the front runner.

Wilbert Robinson

BROOKLYN, N.L. · 1925

Wilbert Robinson was the founder and charter member of the Bonehead Club of Ebbets Field. You would think that anyone in a Dodger uniform back then would automatically qualify for membership, but manager Robinson decided to formalize it by setting certain requirements.

The idea was to cut down on the blundering and cavorting on the field that were the trademarks of the Bums. The rules were simple. Every time a player pulled a boner he put $10 in the pot and joined the Bonehead Club. Robinson figured that given a typical Dodger season, by the end of the year they would have more money in the pot than they would get from the winner's share of the World Series take—assuming they made it that far.

George Brace Photo

Great idea! But it didn't last out the day. Robinson called the whole thing off after he handed the umpires the wrong lineup card at the start of the game and had to ante up the first ten bucks!

Charlie Grimm

CHICAGO, N.L. · OCT. 7, 1935

Jolly Cholly Grimm was a big-hearted fellow. He was so generous he helped give the Detroit Tigers the 1935 World Series championship. There's nothing wrong with that except that he was manager of the opposing Chicago Cubs at the time.

Grimm earned his MBA from The Baseball Hall of SHAME in the climactic sixth game at Detroit with the Tigers leading the Series three games to two.

In the top of the ninth of a 3–3 game, the Cubs' Stan Hack led off with a solid triple. Things looked bright for the Cubs with a runner on third and no outs. All they needed was a sacrifice fly to take the lead and then hold on in the last of the ninth to tie up the Series and force a seventh game.

The next batter, Billy Jurges, struck out. Still, with only one away, the Cubs were in good shape to score. Weary Larry French, who had pitched the entire game, was the next scheduled hitter. Every manager from Little League on up knew what Grimm should do next—bring in a pinch hitter, someone who knew how to handle a bat and advance the runner. Despite a strong bullpen, solid bench strength, and conventional wisdom, Grimm let French bat.

Predictably, the weak-hitting pitcher tapped back to the mound. Hack on third base had no choice but to hold as French was thrown out. Augie Galen then flew out to end the inning and kill any chance of scoring.

In the last of the ninth, the Tigers scored the one run they needed to win the Series.

Defending his failure to use a pinch hitter, Grimm said after the game, "Who knows, French might have dribbled a run-scoring roller. I still think I was right."

The score proves Grimm was wrong. Very wrong.

Lou Boudreau

CLEVELAND, A.L. · 1942

Lou Boudreau had a cold. Lou Boudreau blew his nose—and the game along with it.

During his rookie year as Cleveland's player-manager, Boudreau came down with the sniffles. He took himself out of the lineup but felt well enough to send signals from the dugout to his third base coach. One of the signals, putting a towel to his face, meant a double steal.

But Boudreau promptly forgot it. During the game, Cleveland's Pat Seerey made it to second base. Sometimes called Fat Pat, the nickname said a lot about Seerey's speed on the base paths. Another Cleveland runner who was just as slow was on first.

That's when Boudreau unthinkingly reached for a towel to blow his runny nose. The next thing the young manager knew, Fat Pat lumbered toward third while his teammate plodded toward second. The only ones in the stadium more stunned than Boudreau were the opposing infielders who never expected to be handed such a ridiculously easy double play in a game the Indians eventually lost.

Boudreau barked at coach Oscar "Spinach" Melillo for putting on such a stupid play "with those truck horses on base." Melillo calmly explained that it was Boudreau who gave the signal—and then blew it.

Chuck Dressen

BROOKLYN, N.L. · OCT. 3, 1951

Bobby Thomson would like to publicly thank Chuck Dressen. Dodger fans would settle for a lynching. Dressen's dumb move in the dramatic third game of the National League playoff against the Giants provided the ammunition for "the shot heard 'round the world." It was also the shot that killed the Dodgers' pennant hopes.

Remember? It was the last of the ninth, Dodgers leading 4–2. But the Giants, with only one out, had runners on second and third as home run threat Bobby Thomson strode to the plate.

Dressen called time to talk to the tiring Don Newcombe and decided to make a pitching change. In the Dodger bullpen waited Carl Erskine, Clem Labine and Ralph Branca. Dressen pondered a moment and then made the worst managerial decision of his life. He signaled for Branca.

Why Branca? Didn't Dressen realize that Branca had served a gopher ball to Thomson in the first playoff game? Didn't Dressen realize the Giants had already beaten Branca six times that very year? Didn't Dressen realize the Giants had smashed 11 homers off Branca that season? Apparently not.

In came Branca and out went Thomson's homer.

Hey, Chuck. Couple of guys from Brooklyn out here in the alley wanna talk to you.

The Mean Team

The Meanest Players of All Time

Some players are just plain mean. They play as though they left their consciences in the clubhouse. Their actions on and off the field are so heartless they make Attilla the Hun look like a wimp. They don't walk around with just chips on their shoulders—they carry 2x4s. Maybe they are not so bad once you get to know them ... but why bother? For "The Meanest Players of All Time," The Baseball Hall of SHAME inducts the following:

Billy Martin

INFIELDER · NEW YORK-KANSAS CITY-DETROIT-CLEVELAND-MINNESOTA, A.L.
CINCINNATI-MILWAUKEE, N.L. · 1950–61

MANAGER · MINNESOTA-DETROIT-TEXAS-NEW YORK-OAKLAND, A.L.
1969–82

If ever there was a player who has given the sport a black eye, it's Billy, simply because he's given more than his share of black eyes. He's been miscast as a ballplayer. He's a brawl player.

During a game in 1952 when he was a Yankee second baseman, Billy decided to forgo a simple tag on runner Clint Courtney of the St. Louis

Browns. Instead, Billy, using his gloved hand, viciously swiped at Courtney's face, knocking off the runner's glasses. The obligatory brawl ensued.

Later that same year, Billy duked it out with Jimmy Piersall of the Red Sox twice. One of the fights took place under the stands at Fenway Park. Piersall learned to look up to Billy—after being knocked down twice. The following year, Martin fought a rematch with Courtney during a game against the Browns. It cost both players $150 each in fines.

In 1957, guess who was in the middle of a donnybrook between the Yankees and the White Sox? He was one of five players banished from the game for fisticuffs and assessed another $150 fine.

But the real low blow—his infamous sucker punch—was delivered on Aug. 4, 1960, after he "accidentally" threw his bat at Cub pitcher Jim Brewer. As he went out to retrieve it, Billy suddenly cold-cocked the pitcher and put him in the hospital for several weeks.

In 1969, Billy beat up another pitcher—on his own team. Billy was managing the Minnesota Twins at the time. On August 6, pitcher Dave Boswell and teammate Bob Allison were arguing in a parking lot outside the Lindell Athletic Club in Detroit when Martin jumped in to break it up—and busted up Boswell.

Billy claimed he had been attacked first and added: "I just held on and then started hitting him in the stomach. I worked up and hit him in the mouth, nose and eyes. He bounced off the wall and I hit him again and he was out cold before he hit the ground." Not something to be proud of, but Billy likes to brag about things like that. Boswell was carted off to the hospital where it took 20 stitches to put his face back together. Billy needed seven stitches. In his fist.

Billy has slugged it out with civilians too. In November, 1978, Billy abruptly ended an interview with a reporter for the *Nevada State Journal* by punching the guy's lights out. He didn't like the questions reporter Ray Hagar was asking and tried to grab the notes out of his hand. When Hagar refused to give up his property, Billy hit him "several times." Hagar suffered a gash over one eye and three chipped teeth. Billy's excuse this time? Same as before: "I didn't know him, never punched a writer before . . . I threw it because he was going to punch me first."

The next year, as the Yankee manager, Billy took out his anger and frustration on 52-year-old marshmallow salesman Joseph Cooper. The two met in a bar in Minneapolis on October 23. Cooper went from the bar to the hospital for 15 stitches to close a split lip. Billy said Cooper fell down. The cops said Billy punched him. The Yankees said that's enough and fired Martin. Later, Cooper said the two had been arguing about baseball. Billy didn't like Cooper's views—so he sucker-punched him.

Ty Cobb

OUTFIELDER · DETROIT-PHILADELPHIA, A.L. · 1905–28

It's not true that everyone disliked Ty Cobb. They hated him.

Easily one of the most despised men in baseball, he was called selfish, mean, egotistical, belligerent, and racist. Those were the compliments. Coming in spikes high, ready to slash to ribbons anybody who blocked him from the bag, that was Cobb on his good days.

At his peak he terrorized everyone. Even umpires. Once, he didn't agree with a call by Billy Evans and dared the umpire to meet him under the Detroit stands. "I fight to kill," Cobb warned Evans. And he meant it. The fight that followed was one of the fiercest in baseball history. The two gouged, kicked, punched and clawed for an hour and even though Evans had boxed in college, he couldn't match the nasty street fighter in Cobb. Billy survived only because onlookers dragged an enraged Cobb off the bloodied umpire.

During spring training in 1917, he unleashed the same fury on New York Giants second baseman Buck Herzog. After Cobb reached first in a tune-up game, Herzog dared him to "... come on down if you got any guts." That was mistake number one. Number two was staying in the same ballpark with Cobb. On the next pitch Cobb went into second, spikes flashing, and sliced open Herzog's thigh. That started a fight. They were pulled apart but went at it again that night at the hotel. Herzog got off the first punch, but Cobb came off the floor and pounded him unmercifully.

Cobb's mean streak spread from the field to the stands. Since his vicious playing style triggered the wrath of fans, the razzing he was getting in New York on May 15, 1912, was nothing out of the ordinary. But on this day he was too testy. He jumped into the stands, singled out one fan and started beating him.

The victim was Claude Lucker, who had lost one hand and part of another in an industrial accident. Lucker himself described the gruesome scene when Cobb vaulted into the stands. "He struck me with his fists on the forehead over the left eye and knocked me down. Then he jumped on me and spiked me in the left leg, and kicked me in the side, after which he booted me behind the left ear. I was down and Cobb was kicking me when someone in the crowd shouted: 'Don't kick him! He has no hands!' Cobb answered: 'I don't care if he has no feet!'" The beating sparked a riot and led to the infamous Detroit players' one-game strike in protest of Cobb's suspension.

Cobb was just as vile off the field. Even in a time when bigotry was tolerated and the ban on blacks in baseball was at its strongest, Cobb's virulent racism shocked even the ordinary, garden variety bigots. It reached an incredible extreme during an exhibition tour when he refused to room with Babe Ruth because he had heard a rumor that Ruth had black blood.

Age did nothing to mellow Cobb. He was still just as savage 20 years after he retired. Once he and an ex-big league catcher named Nig Clarke were reminiscing about the old days.

Clarke recalled how he had tricked umpires into calling runners out at the plate by pretending to tag them. "In fact," Clarke confessed to Cobb with a chuckle, "there must have been at least a dozen times when I missed you, but you were called out."

Snarling with fury, Cobb leaped at Clarke's throat and only the efforts of three men who pulled Cobb off saved Clarke from a ferocious beating.

As the years went by, the few friends Cobb had faded away. When he died in 1961 only three men from organized baseball attended his funeral.

Joe Medwick

OUTFIELDER · ST. LOUIS-BROOKLYN-NEW YORK, N.L. · 1932–48

Ducky Medwick hated his own teammates as well as other players in the league. He fought them all.

The hottest temper on the pugnacious Gas House Gang, Medwick rarely wasted time arguing. He just punched first and ended the fight before it even started. Dizzy Dean, who was no shrinking violet himself, had numerous clashes with Medwick. "Joe wops you and the fight is over. That ain't no way to fight," Dizzy complained.

In 1935, Cardinals relief pitcher Ed Heusser got a mouthful of knuckles when he sarcastically suggested to Ducky that he hadn't hustled hard enough in the outfield. Medwick didn't debate the point. He just cold-cocked his own pitcher and the Cardinals had to bring in a reliever.

Another time Cardinals pitcher Tex Carleton was slow getting out of the batting cage before a game while Ducky was waiting to hit. One Medwick punch later, Carleton hurriedly left the cage and took his black eye with him.

During spring training one year, Ducky showed he could just as quickly put an end to a fight that wasn't even his own. Dizzy Dean was complaining to columnist Irv Kupcinet about an item that had appeared in the paper. As the two stood shouting at each other in the hotel lobby, Medwick walked over and with one shot knocked out Kupcinet. End of argument.

Medwick's raging temper helped create the near riot that marred the 1934 World Series. During the seventh game, he slid in high at third and almost disemboweled Tiger third sacker Marvin Owen who retaliated by stomping on Medwick. The inevitable bench-clearing brawl followed and when Ducky returned to his outfield post in the next inning, he was pelted with vegetables, bottles, and seat cushions. No sooner would the ground crew clean up the mess than the barrage started again. Finally, to restore order and to get the game completed, Commissioner Kenesaw Mountain Landis ordered Medwick to the bench.

Stan Williams

PITCHER · LOS ANGELES-ST. LOUIS, N.L.
NEW YORK-CLEVELAND-MINNESOTA-BOSTON, A.L. · 1958–72

Stan Williams had a nasty habit when any batter tried to dig in against him. He reared back and—with all the power of his six-foot, four-inch, 225-pound frame—threw right at their heads. That sort of meanness earned Williams his reputation as a cold-hearted headhunter. Batters had to hit him before he hit them.

Early in his career, Williams beaned Henry Aaron with a fast ball off the helmet. Aaron got to his feet groggy but alive. After the game, Williams approached Aaron and said, "Sorry I hit you on the helmet." Aaron, pleased that the pitcher had shown some concern for his welfare, replied, "That's OK, Stan. Forget it." Snapped Williams, "I meant to hit you in the neck!"

The fact that Williams threw at Aaron wasn't surprising. Hammerin' Hank was such a favorite target, in fact, that Williams kept a picture of Aaron hanging near his locker and threw baseballs at it to keep in practice.

Williams also carried around a little black book filled with the names of the batters he faced. Four stars beside a name meant they were targeted for a pitch where it hurt. As each player felt the sting of a Williams' fast ball, his name was scratched off the list.

When Daryl Spencer was traded to the Dodgers in 1961, Williams thought about removing his new teammate's name from the hit list. "On second thought," Williams told Spencer, "I think I'll keep your name there. You'll probably get traded again."

Along with his meanness, Williams could carry a grudge around for years. When Barry Latman was pitching for the White Sox, he once gave Williams a dose of his own medicine by hitting him with a pitch during a spring training game. Naturally, Latman's name was boldly marked for revenge with the four stars in the little black book. Williams didn't get his chance until years later when both he and Latman were coaches on the same minor league team. Williams was pitching batting practice and when Latman stepped in for his swings, Williams hit him.

Odious Owners

The Most Atrocious Owners in Baseball History

Owners run the baseball teams ... sometimes right into the ground. Through the years, bad owners have shared a common legacy: They view their teams as something to play with and wreck, like electric trains. Their knowledge of the game couldn't fill the inside of a resin bag yet when their team loses, they take it personally—and also out on their players. Above all, these owners see red when that's the color of the numbers on the bottom line. For "The Most Atrocious Owners in Baseball History," The Baseball Hall of SHAME inducts the following:

George Steinbrenner
NEW YORK, A.L. · 1973–PRESENT

Revolutions have been won with less bloodshed, human rights violations, and atrocities than that which have been inflicted on the Yankees during George Steinbrenner's reign of terror.

To baseball, he is a fireman with a torch, an architect with a wrecking ball, a missionary with a machine gun. No one on the team escapes unscathed and, like the law of the jungle, only the strong survive.

He's a millionaire many times over but to measure the value of an owner, you must listen to what the fans have to say. On April 27, 1982, a crowd of 35,000 at Yankee Stadium rose to its feet and broke into a spontaneous chant: "Steinbrenner sucks! Steinbrenner sucks!"

No sooner was George III settled on the throne as the Yankee owner than he was forced to abdicate his kingdom. In 1974, after he was convicted

of making an illegal campaign contribution to President Nixon's reelection committee and fined $15,000, George was suspended by Commissioner Bowie Kuhn from operating the Yankee franchise for 15 months. But wily George still managed to browbeat his players even in exile.

The players were forced to sit and listen as a tape recorder spewed out his mean, vindictive messages. One of his milder tirades was: "I'll be a son-of-a-bitch if I'm going to sit up here and sign these paychecks and watch us get our asses kicked by a bunch of rummies!"

At times, Steinbrenner's personal attacks damaged careers and reputations. Pitcher Jim Beattie was one who suffered the aftereffects of a Steinbrenner temper tantrum.

In 1978 against Boston, Beattie was knocked out of the game in the third inning and optioned to the minors by the sixth inning. Steinbrenner callously claimed that Beattie "lacked the guts" to pitch for the Yankees.

But that's part of Steinbrenner's pattern. For years, he has used the Yankees' International League farm team in Columbus, Ohio, as his personal Siberia. Players who earned his disfavor found themselves on the New York to Columbus shuttle. In 1981, pitcher Mike Griffin gave up five runs to the Mets in an exhibition game and his next pitching assignment was in Columbus. The next year, third baseman Tucker Ashford made two errors—also in an exhibition game. "We've seen enough of Ashford," George announced and guess where Ashford went? Pitcher Dave LaRoche learned how to find Ohio with his eyes closed. He made four round trips between New York and Columbus in 1982.

George seems to get nastier with age. Early in the 1984 season, rookie shortstop Bobby Meacham made an eighth-inning miscue that allowed the winning run to score in a 7–6 loss. So Steinbrenner sent Bobby packing for the minors. However, George didn't just ship Meacham back to Columbus. Instead he kicked the rookie *two* rungs down the minor league ladder to Nashville (Class AA).

Yankee managers are treated with similar kindness. They have about as much job security as a Bolivian president. They get a gold watch if they can last out a year. The sound most often heard in the clubhouse is the revolving door marked "Managers Only."

Since he took over the front office in 1973, George has gone through enough managers to fill Yankee Stadium. It seems the Yankee chieftain hires managers just so he can enjoy the pleasure of firing them. The record speaks for itself:

- Jan. 23, 1974. Bill Virdon hired as manager to replace Ralph Houk.
- Aug. 1, 1975. Virdon fired. Billy Martin hired.
- July 25, 1978. Martin resigned under fire. Bob Lemon hired.
- June 18, 1979. Lemon fired. Martin hired.
- Oct. 28, 1979. Martin fired. Dick Howser hired.
- Nov. 21, 1980. Howser fired. Gene Michael hired.
- Sept. 6, 1981. Michael fired. Lemon hired.
- April 25, 1982. Lemon fired. Michael hired.
- Aug. 3, 1982. Michael fired. Clyde King hired.
- Jan. 11, 1983. King transferred. Martin hired.
- Dec. 16, 1983. Martin fired. Yogi Berra hired.
- To be continued.

Charles O. Finley
KANSAS CITY-OAKLAND, A.L. · 1960–80

Charles O. Finley was one of the most outrageous owners ever to curdle the milk of human kindness.

The insurance magnate knew as much about baseball as he did about nuclear physics—nothing—but that didn't stop him from phoning his managers and telling them how to manage. He went a step further and had the gall to tell his players how to play.

At times, he sauntered into the Athletics clubhouse and, with the air of a baron lording over his serfs, read unflattering descriptions of his team to his players. He also humiliated his managers by berating them in their office—with the door open for all to hear.

But that kind of contempt for his players was an old Finley trademark. He first showed it in his early days as owner when the A's were still in Kansas City. As one of his self-promotion gimmicks, Finley brought a herd of mules to the stadium and to the everlasting humiliation of his starting lineup, forced his players to parade around the stadium in single file mounted on mule back!

Nothing more clearly revealed the devious way Finley operated than his treatment of A's reserve second baseman Mike Andrews during the 1973 World Series against the Mets.

Andrews committed back-to-back errors in the twelfth inning that allowed the Mets to score four runs and win the game 10–7. Finley was furious. He tried to coerce Andrews into signing a statement that would put the player on the disabled list and thus disqualify him for the rest of the Series. The rest of the team threatened open revolt if Andrews was declared disabled. The press screamed over the unfair treatment. Even Commissioner Bowie Kuhn couldn't ignore such a flagrant violation of a player's rights. The next day he ruled that Andrews had to be reinstated immediately, publicly scolded Finley and slapped him with a $5,000 fine for his interference.

But since there was nothing that said the A's *had* to play Andrews, Finley ordered that the player be benched for the rest of the Series. As soon as the season was over, Finley handed Andrews his unconditional release. Andrews never played in the majors again.

Manager Dick Williams, unable to stomach Finley's meddling any longer, resigned. Snapped Williams: "Finley likes to have everyone in his employ—and I mean everyone from the manager to the shoeshine boy—under his thumb. Then he pushes as hard as he can to keep them down."

Over the next few years, Finley acted like an emperor who had turned his cannons on his kingdom. Seldom in the history of the game had one owner so totally destroyed a dynasty as had Finley. He peddled off or surrendered to free agency stars like Reggie Jackson, Rollie Fingers, and Joe Rudi who had brought him five division titles and three World Series championships.

By 1977, just two years after winning a division title, the A's plunged to the cellar with a dismal 54–108 record.

Finley continued to meddle in the field management of the team usually by long distance phone calls from his ivory tower in Chicago where he lived. In 1979, he showed how little he cared about his team by not attending a single game—even when the A's were playing in Chicago.

Andrew Freedman

NEW YORK, N.L. · 1895–1902

Today's megabuck players who whine about their contract and run to arbitration if an owner so much as frowns at them never had it so good. A complaint to owner Andrew Freedman was worth a quick clout in the chops—if Freedman happened to be in a gentle mood that day.

Unquestionably, Freedman was the most despised owner in baseball, a vain, arrogant, cruel man. He beat up fans, umps, other owners—even his own players.

He used the millions he made in real estate (aided by his cozy connections with corrupt Tammany Hall) to purchase the Giants. And baseball in New York entered a long nightmare.

Despite his wealth, Freedman was a classic tightwad. His cheapness was like a rope around the neck that slowly strangled the once powerful Giants. He sold off the high-priced players and fired any manager who wouldn't toe his dictatorial line. Thirteen field managers came and went during the seven-year run of the Freedman Follies. He hired one skipper right out of a circus business office where one of his major duties involved feeding the fish.

Freedman literally terrorized his team. When a player displeased him, he stormed into the clubhouse and punched out the hapless offender. Often, Freedman was surrounded by his handpicked stadium police who had been conveniently assigned to duty at the Polo Grounds by the Tammany Hall politicians.

He carried on bitter feuds with anyone who crossed him—fans, umpires, players, managers, sportswriters, even rival owners, one of whom he attacked and mauled with his bare hands. The victim was pounded severely and ended up in the hospital. A number of times, umpires who made calls that angered Freedman were barred from the Polo Grounds on his orders. He tried the same thing with a sportswriter but lost that round in court when the reporter sued.

When Oriole Ducky Holmes, a former player of his, responded to the taunting crowd with a crack about Freedman, the owner charged out of the stands with his personal storm troopers backing him up. He tried to have Ducky dragged out of the park. The umpires refused to allow it and threatened to forfeit the game to Baltimore if Freedman didn't get off the field. Freedman continued screaming and cursing. The umpires had no choice but to call the forfeit.

Freedman tried to ruin the career of one of the most popular players of the day. Giants pitcher Amos Rusie had won 29 or more games five years straight, including 36 in 1894. But in 1895 Freedman started whittling away at his $3,000 salary with ridiculous and undeserved fines because

Rusie's record had fallen to 22–21. When Rusie asked for a raise to $5,000 the following season, Freedman retorted with a nasty laugh: "I have offered Rusie $2,400 and unless he signs and gets down to business, he will not play ball at all." Rusie rejected the insulting offer and sat out the '96 season. He came back in 1897 only because the other owners, missing his drawing power at the box office, chipped in to boost his salary. That year Rusie won 29 and lost 8.

The Rusie situation was just one more shoddy episode in Freedman's rapidly accumulating bag of disgraces. Freedman's shocking contempt for baseball, its players and its tradition got to be too much for the other owners. They took a vote and forced him to sell his interest in the Giants and get out of baseball. For good.

Christian Frederick Wilhelm von der Ahe
ST. LOUIS, N.L. · 1882–98

Chris von der Ahe was the Clown Prince of the Diamond Dolts.

Chris looked like he had leaped straight from the Katzenjammer Kids comic strip into real life. His loutish manners and his thick accent ("I am der boss president of der Prowns!") enhanced the image. He favored loud checkered suits and a squashed-down derby hat whether touring his breweries or his ballpark. According to one contemporary description, von der Ahe was ". . . a big man with a face like the full moon and a nose like a bunch of strawberries. It's a wonder he wasn't cross-eyed from trying to see around it. He had a stomach as big as a bush leaguer's opinion of himself and for every step he took forward he had to take two to each side."

Chris, owner of a brewery in St. Louis, bought the ball club and named it the Browns for no other reason other than that the uniforms were brown. He took an active role in running the team although his ignorance of the game was unbelievable. For a time he bragged about owning the biggest diamond in baseball and seemed confused when told all baseball diamonds were the same size. During an owners meeting, he scolded his colleagues for scheduling too many rainy days in St. Louis and demanded that Chicago and Cincinnati get their share.

To the lasting mortification of his players, "der boss president" accompanied them on road trips and insisted they march behind him in single file from the railroad station to the hotel.

Never at a loss for words, von der Ahe indiscriminately called all his competitors thieves, crooks, and robbers. He also lambasted his own players.

Von der Ahe favored a seat in the dugout where he followed the flight of the ball with a telescope. He hated fly balls as much as he disliked teetotalers. Players who popped up were loudly flayed: "Stop hitting them high fliers," he screamed. "Keep them on the floor! Don't you know them fielders can catch them high vuns?"

Under von der Ahe's heavy hand, the club started coming apart. He peddled off most of his best players to Brooklyn. Then he started going through managers like hops through a vat of beer. Seven came and went in one year. But Chris still wasn't satisfied. He took over running the team himself and for the Browns that meant a one-way ticket to Losersville. Any player who committed an error on the field could count on a good cussing out in the clubhouse from "der boss president."

Von der Ahe's ruination was inevitable, but he hastened it along by turning the ballpark into sort of a Coney Island West and making baseball part of the absurdity. The beer garden outside the gate was fine, but when horse racing and a shoot-the-chute boat ride from a high tower into an artificial lake were set up next to the ballpark, the baseball fans in St. Louis had had enough.

Von der Ahe's eccentricities drove the Browns into bankruptcy and he sold out. He ended up in a job ideally suited to his nature—bartending in a grubby little saloon.

Chris von der Ahe did leave an important legacy. He introduced the hot dog to baseball. It was very fitting since he was one himself.

Foul Bawls

The Worst Excuses for Missing a Game or Blowing a Play

Excuses are like artsy films—you admire their originality but they wear pretty thin after the first ten minutes. Some ballplayers have an uncanny knack for conjuring up creative reasons why it's not their fault that they can't catch a fly ball or get a hit. And when they need an excuse to stay out of the lineup, they're as adept as a juvenile delinquent playing hooky. For "The Worst Excuses for Missing a Game or Blowing a Play," The Baseball Hall of SHAME inducts the following:

Jose Cardenal

OUTFIELDER
SAN FRANCISCO-ST. LOUIS-CHICAGO- PHILADELPHIA-NEW YORK, N.L.
CALIFORNIA-CLEVELAND-KANSAS CITY, A.L. · 1963–80

Even if Jose hadn't been a decent outfielder, he'd have been worth keeping on the roster just for his wonderfully imaginative excuses.

Jose was the type who, if he couldn't give 100 percent effort on the field, thought it best not to give any. So he often drove his managers crazy with his reasons why he belonged in the comfort of the dugout rather than out in the hot sun.

Before one road game in 1972, Jose took himself out of the Cubs lineup because of "crickets." His incredulous manager, Whitey Lockman,

asked for a better explanation, all the while anticipating an excuse straight from left field. Jose said crickets in his hotel room the night before had made so much noise he couldn't sleep and now he was too tired to play in the game.

Jose topped that beaut in 1974 when he decided to take it easy on the bench for a few games. The reason this time? His eyelid was stuck open!

Lou Novikoff

OUTFIELDER · CHICAGO, N.L. · 1941–44

They didn't call him "The Mad Russian" for nothing. That's "mad" as in totally bananas.

Anytime a ball was hit over his head in Wrigley Field, Novikoff would back up only so far and go no farther. More often than not, the ball bounced off the wall and shot past him back toward the infield.

Why did he constantly give up on those catchable long drives? Because, as Novikoff explained to beleaguered Chicago Cubs manager Charlie Grimm, he had an incredible fear of vines! That can be a real problem when you're playing in the ivy-covered confines of Wrigley Field.

Grimm tried everything he could think of to cure Novikoff of his fear of vines. He brought in poisonous goldenrod to show the outfielder that the vines were not goldenrod. Grimm even rubbed the Wrigley vines all over his own face and hands and then chewed a few to prove it wasn't poison ivy. But Novikoff never did get over his aversion to vines. Consequently, a lot of balls sailed over his head.

And if that excuse got a little weak, he had another cooked up to explain away his terrible fielding. "I can't play in Wrigley," he complained to Grimm, "because the left field line isn't straight like it is in other parks. It's crooked."

Charles "Flint" Rhem

PITCHER · ST. LOUIS, N.L. · SEPT. 19, 1930

The Cardinals were battling their way to the pennant in 1930. It was a tight race with the Cubs, the Giants, and the Dodgers all challenging. The Redbirds needed every victory they could get their hands on and they depended on a strong, healthy pitching staff. Flint Rhem was one of their steady pitchers.

George Brace Photo

But during a crucial series with the Dodgers, Rhem disappeared without a word of explanation. Flint was gone for over 48 hours and the St. Louis management was beginning to fear the worst about their big right hander.

Then just as suddenly as he vanished, Rhem reappeared, mystified by all the commotion he'd caused. There was a simple explanation for his disappearing act, he reported. Gangsters had kidnapped him! Yes, and not only that but they had held him prisoner at gunpoint and forced him, totally against his will, to consume massive amounts of demon rum!

Manager Gabby Street and General Manager Branch Rickey needed Flint so they could only look at one another and shake their heads. "We were in no position to disprove Rhem's story," said Rickey.

Billy Loes

PITCHER · BROOKLYN, N.L. · OCT. 6, 1952

The Dodgers' Billy Loes was pitching more excuses than fast balls during the 1952 World Series.

He hurled his best alibis in the seventh inning of the sixth game against the Yankees. The Dodgers were winning 1–0, but the Yanks had a runner on first when Loes went into his stretch and dropped the ball to commit a balk. Later he explained that the ball just squirted out of his hands because there was "too much spit on it."

That was bad enough, but even worse was the excuse he gave for the play that followed. With a runner in scoring position, weak-hitting pitcher Vic Raschi hit an easy grounder back to the mound. Loes didn't get his glove down in time and the ball bounced off his knee for an RBI single. The Dodgers lost, 3–2. Loes' alibi for missing the grounder: "I lost it in the sun."

Even before the Series began, Loes tried to weasel out of a touchy situation with a lame excuse. Trouble erupted when a newspaper quoted him saying that the Yankees would beat his Dodgers in six games. That wasn't the brightest thing to say about a team you're pitching for. When Chuck Dressen, the Brooklyn manager, read him the riot act for his stupid statements, Loes blamed the reporter. "I told him the Yankees would win in seven," he said, "but he screwed it up and had me saying they would win it in six!"

George Brace Photo

Mascot Madness

The Most Tasteless Team Mascots

There are some things the world could do just fine without. War ... famine ... pestilence ... baseball mascots. Who needs them? Fans go to the ballpark to watch the game, not some waddling, squawking, Sesame Street-type mutant. What's with all these over-grown chickens, parrots, and Fred-Birds? Are they some new zoo-logical species waiting to be classified? For "The Most Tasteless Team Mascots," The Baseball Hall of SHAME inducts the following:

Chicago White Stockings' Black Mascot

1888

On an around-the-world tour with the White Stockings, Albert Spalding and Cap Anson took along a mascot that symbolized American bigotry at its worst. For baseball and the country, it was a shameful episode devoid of any human dignity.

Cap Anson, player-manager of the Chicago team, was a pioneer in American baseball. He was also its most vicious racist, partly responsible for setting the color line in baseball.

Spalding was just as bigoted in his own right, but compounded that shameful trait with his cynical exploitation of baseball as a means of selling more of his sporting goods. To promote sales, he organized the world tour of the White Stockings.

Despite the Emancipation Proclamation, Spalding and Anson took along on the tour their own version of neo-slavery in the person of Clarence Duval, a black youth they hypocritically called their "mascot" but who was little more than an indentured servant.

Duval was forced into a degrading, stereotypical Stepin Fetchit role that would be an embarrassment today to any sensitive American. He was patronized by the press as a "... slenderly built, impish-faced Negro with a remarkable talent for plantation dancing and baton twirling." The press didn't spell out that the mascot scratched his head, shuffled his feet and acted the fool, but those were the public duties expected of Spalding's and Anson's "boy."

Before each game, Spalding made sure his mascot was decked out in a comic-opera bright red coat with gold lace and white trousers stuffed into patent leather boots. His job was simple—and degrading. Strutting and prancing, Duval led the team onto the field and then went into his demonstration of "plantation dancing."

When the tour was over, so was Duval's usefulness to "Massas" Al and Cap. But while Duval was the mascot, he came close to breaking baseball's rigid color line, which existed for the next 60 years.

The San Francisco Crab

SAN FRANCISCO, N.L. · 1984–PRESENT

The Giants pouted for years because everyone else around the league had a silly mascot and they didn't. The Giants needed something, anything, to distract the disgruntled fans from realizing they were paying good money to watch lousy baseball when they could be over on Alcatraz sitting underneath the seagulls for nothing.

So the Giants conducted a poll. They asked their fans what kind of mascot would best represent their team—a chronic cellar dweller scuttling around in one of the worst ballparks in creation. The fans told the Giants precisely what they could do with their dumb idea. Sixty-five percent who bothered answering the question said they didn't want any mascot at all. With such a clear mandate from their fans, the Giants picked out a mascot anyway.

The Giants chose a crab. And not just any crab, mind you, but a sordid, slimy, yucky-looking creature that slinks around Candlestick Park.

To the fans, it instantly became the symbol of second class, second division losers everywhere. They love the repulsive thing—love to degrade it. Whenever it creeps out into the light during the changing of sides in

the fifth inning, the fans boo it, spit on it, dump beer on it and throw trash at it.

What other kind of treatment would you expect of something that looks like a giant wart with distemper?

Charlie O. The Mule

KANSAS CITY-OAKLAND, A.L. · 1965–77

When Charlie O. Finley introduced his team mascot, people said it takes one to know one. The mascot was a mule named after its owner.

Charlie O., the owner, was a benevolent sort—with his livestock, not with his team. The private pasture and pen he installed for his four-legged alter ego outside the stadium made the players' facilities look like the city dump. Just to make sure Charlie O., the mule, didn't get lonely (and to hold down groundskeepers' expenses), Charlie O., the owner, also imported a flock of sheep complete with shepherd to graze the right field expanse and keep the grass down.

But Charlie O., the owner, was also generous to a fault with the other teams who came to town. He was fond of sharing Charlie O., the mule, by parading him in front of the visitors' dugout and bullpen just before the game and just after the creature had consumed a particularly heavy meal. Obliging the boss, Charlie O., the mule, would then deposit fragrant mementoes which the visitors took home with them—if they couldn't get their spikes clean.

Booing the Boo Birds

The Most Unruly Behavior of Fans

Fans come to the ball park to watch a game and engage in one of America's favorite pastimes—booing. At the ump, the gopher-ball pitcher, the slumping slugger. But sometimes the real boos shouldn't be directed at the playing field but right up in the stands, where fans have displayed some of the rudest, raunchiest, rowdiest behavior this side of a riot zone. For "The Most Unruly Behavior of Fans," The Baseball Hall of SHAME inducts the following:

Montreal Expo Fans

JULY 28, 1983

The Expo fans in Olympic Stadium sank to a new low in crudeness. Their boos and jeers weren't directed at any of the Expos or their opponents or even the umpires. No, these fans picked on the *wife* of one of the players and drove her from the field in tears.

Because of his lousy relief work on the mound, Expo pitcher Jeff Reardon had fallen into disfavor with the fans. Taking umbrage over his failure to hold late-inning leads, the fans began riding and even booing him from the moment he left the bullpen for the walk to the mound.

That's all part of the game, but the fans crossed the line of just plain meanness during ceremonies between games of a double-header with the Cardinals.

Reardon's wife Phebe was among several players' wives making an appearance on the field in connection with a food drive for the poor. As she was introduced, the mere mention of the name Reardon triggered a ragged chorus of boos that grew in intensity. As the booing reached a crescendo, Mrs. Reardon fled from the field in tears and embarrassment.

But the shame wasn't hers. It belonged exclusively to the booing fans in Montreal.

Frank Kuraczea, Jr.

YANKEE FAN · OCT. 9, 1981

The cry of "Kill the Umpire!" is as old as baseball itself. Fans don't really mean it—although some act as if they do.

During a playoff game between the Milwaukee Brewers and the New York Yankees at Yankee Stadium, third base umpire Mike Reilly called Yankee Dave Winfield out in a close play at the bag in the sixth inning.

Fan Frank Kuraczea, sitting in the stands near third, thought Winfield was safe. After the Yankees took their positions on the field for the top of the seventh, Kuraczea was still so incensed that he vaulted over the low wall and pounced on Reilly's back in front of 54,000 stunned witnesses. The pair fell to the ground as Kuraczea began swinging and cursing.

Yankee third baseman Graig Nettles grabbed the enraged fan from behind. Within seconds, other players and stadium security officers dove into the pile. It took four burly cops to drag Kuraczea into the nearby dugout. Once they had wrestled him to the floor, they found a blackjack in his back pocket. The Ansonia, Connecticut, resident was hauled off to the police station and charged with illegal possession of a dangerous weapon, criminal trespassing, and disorderly conduct.

Left Field Cincinnati Fans

MAY 12, 1974

Houston outfielder Bob Watson lay crumpled on the warning track in Cincy's Riverfront Stadium after crashing into the left field wall in futile pursuit of a fly ball. He was stunned and barely conscious, his face bleeding and eyes temporarily blinded by pieces of his shattered sunglasses.

About a dozen fans in the front row of the first deck leaned over the railing. Were they concerned? Did they want to offer help? Hell, no. They proceeded to bombard the injured Watson with beer, ice and other debris. Even a Salvadoran guerrilla would have shown more mercy.

"They were like maniacs," Watson later recalled. "I knew glass might be in my right eye and that any tiny movement might scrape my eyeball and cause damage." So the stricken Watson could only lay there helplessly while junk rained down on him.

Teammate Cesar Cedeno was also caught in the barrage from the sick group when he rushed to Watson's aid. "He could have lost an eye," Cedeno said angrily. "And those damn fans were laughing and throwing beer and stuff down on us and calling us all kinds of names."

The repulsive fans battled security guards who finally dragged them away kicking and screaming.

Although Watson didn't press charges, he did get a small taste of poetic justice. While he was being treated for his injuries, three of the rowdies showed up at the same hospital for stitches to the cracked heads they received—apparently from beating their heads on the cops' nightsticks.

Cleveland Indian Fans
SEPT. 27, 1940

The fans in the cheap seats at Municipal Stadium got downright vicious when the Detroit Tigers came to town for a crucial three-game series with second place Cleveland. The Tigers needed only one more victory to clinch the pennant.

It was Ladies Day but the 40,000-plus fans in the stands made it look more like a convention of produce peddlers. They brought with them fruits and vegetables—which weren't for eating.

In the first inning, Detroit got a taste of what was coming when Hank Greenberg, circling under a fly ball in left field, was nearly buried in a shower of produce from the stands.

Umpire Bill Summers then announced over the public address system that any further disturbances would result in a forfeit—one which would hand the pennant to the Tigers.

Meanwhile, stadium police were roving through the crowd, grabbing the worst offenders and hustling them out. As the cops approached a particularly rowdy group in the upper deck, one of the troublemakers threw all his ammunition—tomatoes, eggs, bottles, and other assorted trash—into one basket and tossed it over the side into the Tiger bullpen. The basket landed right on the head of Detroit catcher Birdie Tebbetts. He was knocked out cold.

When he was revived, Tebbetts was taken to the clubhouse for treatment. The cops, waiting there with his assailant, asked Tebbetts if he wanted to press charges of assault. Tebbetts, nice guy that he was, declined and said he would settle the matter himself.

Exactly how the fan left the stadium with a busted nose is not quite clear.

New York Giants Fans

APRIL 11, 1907

The fans in the Polo Grounds got the shame, but the weatherman got the blame for the Giants' forfeit of their opening day game to the Phillies— thanks to a wild snowball fight.

Despite an unusually heavy April snowfall, the field had been cleared to play ball on a day that was more suited for football. The game was a bummer for Giant fans. Philadelphia grabbed an early 3–0 lead and held it through eight innings while New York could only muster one hit.

The cold, uncomfortable fans grew progressively more restless. Given the conditions and the tempting piles of snow that had been scraped off the seats, the outcome was inevitable. The only surprise was that the game went all the way through the eighth before the first snowball sailed through the air.

Of course, one good snowball deserves another and within minutes it looked like another blizzard had hit the Polo Grounds. The air turned white as the fans bombarded one another. Naturally, with such inviting and convenient targets down below, their attention soon turned to the Giants, the Phillies and (with happy revenge in their hearts) to the umpires.

Snowballs rained down on the field. The players couldn't tell the snowballs from the baseballs and took refuge in the dugouts. When it was obvious that the man-made snowstorm was not going to let up, umpire Bill Klem ordered the forfeit and the Phillies won 9–0. Snow joke, it really happened.

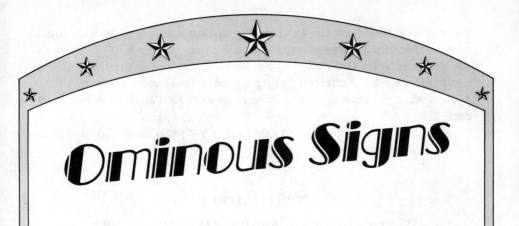

Ominous Signs

The Worst Coaching Blunders

The titles lost, the games blown, and the reputations tarnished aren't always due to the players' goofs. Sometimes the on-field blundering is the result of bubbleheaded coaching from the sidelines. Too often the coaches take a nap while the players take the rap. For "The Worst Coaching Blunders," The Baseball Hall of SHAME inducts the following:

Joe McCarthy

ACTING THIRD BASE COACH · NEW YORK YANKEES
APRIL 26, 1931

Manager Joe McCarthy liked to think of himself as a coach. But he learned he was better off sticking to managing in the dugout after pulling an incredible boner that cost Lou Gehrig the home run crown.

During a game with the Senators, McCarthy took over the coaching chores at third base. At one point, Lyn Lary was on first with Gehrig at bat. Gehrig smashed a drive toward the right center field stands. As Lary rounded second, he glanced toward center and saw outfielder Sam Rice catch the ball. But what Lary missed seeing was that Rice caught the ball after it bounced out of the stands and back onto the field for a home run. Thinking it was the third out to end the inning, Lary crossed third and trotted into the Yankee dugout. Meanwhile, Gehrig rounded the bases certain of his homer, but was called out for passing the base runner. Gehrig thought that Lary had already scored ahead of him.

And where was third base coach Joe McCarthy whose job it was to prevent such blunders? He was jumping up and down, leading the crowd in the cheers for Gehrig's homer—with his back to the field! McCarthy's cheerleading robbed Gehrig of the home run. He was credited with a triple. Even worse, it cheated Gehrig out of an undisputed home run title. At the end of the season, he and Babe Ruth were tied at 46 round-trippers each.

After that game, which the Yankees lost 9–7, McCarthy did his signal calling from the dugout.

Salty Parker

THIRD BASE COACH · HOUSTON, N.L. · SEPT. 22, 1969

It was a tight ball game. The Astros trailed the Braves by the slimmest of margins, 4–3 in the seventh inning. But Houston had the tying run at third.

Base runner Norm Miller inched down the third base line as coach Salty Parker reminded him to be extra careful of a possible pickoff. It was Parker's job to do what he could to help Miller score the tying run.

On the next pitch, Braves pitcher Cecil Upshaw fired a low, outside fastball. Catcher Bob Didier, who was wearing a temporary cast on a finger on his glove hand, lunged for the ball. He caught it but the force of the pitch knocked the white cast loose and sent it spinning end over end toward the backstop.

At least, that's what most everybody in the ball park saw. To Parker, the spinning cast looked like a baseball, a wild pitch that got away.

"Go! Go!" he screamed at Miller. Complying with Parker's orders, Miller raced for home. Too bad for the Astros that he listened to his coach.

If Parker had been on his toes, he would have noticed that Didier hadn't bothered to chase the "wild pitch." Instead, the catcher was standing at the plate with a huge grin on his face—and the ball in his hand— waiting to tag out a dumbfounded Norm Miller. The Astros lost the game ... and had a few salty words for Parker.

Tony Cuccinello

THIRD BASE COACH · CHICAGO, A.L. · OCT. 2, 1959

Tony "Cooch" Cuccinello couldn't tell the difference between a Sherman Lollar and a Sherman tank. Sherman, the ballplayer, was just about as fast as Sherman, the tank, but that didn't matter to Cooch who was coaching at third for the White Sox in the second game of the 1959 World Series against the Los Angeles Dodgers.

Cooch waved his slow-footed runner home on a crucial eighth-inning play that ended with a big out and thwarted a White Sox rally.

The Sox were trailing 4–2 with nobody out in the bottom of the eighth but were threatening with Earl Torgeson on second and catcher Sherm Lollar on first. Al Smith then hit a long drive to left center. Torgeson scored easily but by the time Lollar, who was never known for his speed, came puffing around second, outfielder Wally Moon had already played the carom off the wall and was turning to hit the cutoff man. But there was Cooch in the coach's box windmilling and yelling for Sherm to "Go!" Sherm went but not nearly fast enough. Shortstop Maury Wills took Moon's throw and fired the relay home. By the time Sherm finally chugged to the plate, catcher Johnny Roseboro had been waiting with the ball so long he was ready to draw his pension. Sherm didn't even slide. It would have been useless. Instead of runners at second and third with nobody out and a chance to at least tie, if not beat, the Dodgers, the White Sox had a runner on second and one out. They lost the game 4–3. It was the turning point of the series as the Dodgers went on to beat Chicago four games to two and take the championship.

"I waved him in," Cuccinello admitted. "I'm to blame."

Nobody's arguing, Cooch.

Dreadful Drubbings

The Most Crushing Single Game Defeats

Losing a game is one thing. But getting trounced, trampled, and stomped is a disgrace. It's such a mortifying feeling, much like how the losers felt on the seventh day of the Six Day War. For "The Most Crushing Single Game Defeats," the Baseball Hall of SHAME inducts the following:

Boston Red Sox 29, St. Louis Browns 4

JUNE 8, 1950

No team sank to such a humiliating low as the Browns, who wound up on the short end of the most lopsided score in modern baseball history.

During the long, dismal afternoon in Boston, four Browns pitchers gave up runs as if the game was a bake sale—cheaper by the dozen. The 5,105 fans in Fenway Park roared with delight, not so much for the offensive display of the Red Sox as for the astounding ineptness of the Browns' pitchers. On their way to this monumental rout, the St. Louis pitching staff surrendered the most runs in one game and allowed the most total bases, 60.

The Brownies made losing a new art form. This was no fluke. They began working on a masterpiece drubbing the day before when they were overwhelmed by the Red Sox 20–4.

Twenty-four hours later, the Browns hurlers gave the fans a classic exhibition of throw-and-duck by serving up 28 hits, including nine doubles, seven homers, and a triple.

Browns starter Cliff Fannin got the discredit for the loss. His pitches were hit harder than he threw them as he was shelled for eight runs in the first two innings. The next lamb led to slaughter was pitcher Cuddles Marshall. You would expect the Red Sox to pick on anyone named Cuddles. And they did—with another nine runs in 1⅔ innings. Sid Schacht came to the mound next, lasted 3⅔ innings, and then ran for cover. Tom Ferrick relieved him and, to the relief of everybody, somehow got the last two outs to end the disaster.

Adding further indignity to the Browns pitchers, they had trouble getting out the weakest hitter on the Red Sox, opposing hurler Chuck Stobbs. He collected two hits and walked four straight times.

ST. LOUIS	ab	r	h	po	a	e		BOSTON	ab	r	h	po	a	e
Lenhardt, lf	4	2	2	4	0	0		Vollmer, cf	7	1	1	5	0	0
Kokos, rf	4	1	2	2	0	1		Pesky, 3b	7	3	5	0	1	0
Lollar, c	3	0	1	0	0	0		Williams, lf	5	8	2	4	0	0
Moss, c	1	0	0	2	0	0		Stephens, ss	6	4	3	5	3	0
Sievers, cf	4	0	1	3	0	0		Dropo, 1b	6	5	4	5	1	0
Arft, 1b	3	0	1	5	0	0		Zarilla, rf	7	4	5	0	0	0
Friend, 2b	4	0	1	5	0	0		Doerr, 2b	6	4	4	2	1	0
Upton, ss	3	0	0	1	5	0		Batts, c	6	2	2	6	0	0
Thomas, 3b	3	1	0	2	3	0		Stobbs, p	3	3	2	0	0	0
Fannin, p	0	0	0	0	0	0								
aGarver	1	0	0	0	0	0		Total	53	29	28	27	6	0
Marshall, p	1	0	0	0	0	0								
Schacht, p	2	0	0	0	0	0								
Ferrick, p	0	0	0	0	0	0								
Total	33	4	8	24	8	1								

aStruck out for Fannin in third.

St. Louis   0 0 3 0 0 0 0 0 1 —   4
Boston   0 8 5 7 2 0 2 5 x — 29

Runs batted in—Batts 2, Vollmer 2, Williams 5, Dropo 7, Doerr 8, Stephens 3, Kokos, Sievers 2, Arft, Pesky 2.

Two-base hits—Zarilla 4, Batts, Arft, Stephens, Vollmer, Pesky 2. Three-base hit—Stephens. Home runs—Williams 2, Dropo 2, Doerr 3. Double plays—Dropo (unassisted); Doerr, Stephens and Dropo. Left on bases—St. Louis 10, Boston 11. Bases on balls—Off Fannin 4, Marshall 5, Schacht 2, Stobbs 7. Struck out—By Schacht 2, Stobbs 5. Hits—Off Fannin 7 in 2 innings, Marshall 7 in 1 2-3, Schacht 13 in 3 2-3, Ferrick 1 in 2-3. Hit by pitcher—By Stobbs (Arft). Winning pitcher—Stobbs (4–1). Losing pitcher—Fannin (1–3). Umpires—Hubbard, Rommel and Paparella. Time of game—2:42. Attendance—5,105.

Pittsburgh Pirates 22, Chicago Cubs 0

SEPT. 16, 1975

It was the most appalling shutout slaughter of the twentieth century.

Before they had even managed to get three outs, the Cubs were praying for rain and looking for a hole to hide in at Wrigley Field.

The fans had hardly settled in their seats before starter Rick Reuschel was on his way to the showers after giving up eight runs, six hits, and two walks in only ⅓ inning. The Pirates added another tally in the first and went on to batter Cub pitching for 24 hits. Every single Pirate in the starting lineup collected at least one hit and scored at least one run.

After the first inning, the vendors were selling hot dogs to go. Nobody was more bored by this trouncing than some of the Cubs themselves, especially outfielder Jose Cardenal. He spent most of the time—when not chasing down Pirate extra-base hits—studying the ivy on the outfield wall. "I was watching a spider crawl through the ivy," he said. "What else was there to do out there in a game like that?"

											R	H	E
PITTSBURGH	9	0	2	1	6	2	2	0	0	—	22	24	0
CHICAGO	0	0	0	0	0	0	0	0	0	—	0	3	3

Boston Red Sox 23, Detroit Tigers 3

JUNE 18, 1953

There were no limits to the mortification the Tigers were willing to inflict upon themselves. After getting blown out by the Red Sox 17–1 the day before, the Tigers were bombed by Boston for another 17 runs—only this time in one inning.

It was an annihilation fit for General Custer.

Detroit trailed Boston 5–3 going into the bottom of the seventh inning when the barrage started. The carnage lasted 48 minutes and when the toothless Tigers finally staggered off the field, they carried with them the shameful record of allowing the highest-scoring inning in modern history.

In the inning, three Detroit pitchers combined to face 23 batters before getting three outs. They surrendered 11 singles, two doubles, a home run and six walks. They had no one to blame but themselves. All runs were earned.

											R	H	E
DETROIT	0	0	0	2	0	1	0	0	0	—	3	7	5
BOSTON	0	3	0	0	0	2	17	1	x	—	23	27	0

Brooklyn Dodgers 19, Cincinnati Reds 1

MAY 21, 1952

If this had been a boxing match, the referee would have stopped the fight at the opening bell. But since this was baseball, the Reds had to stick it out even though they suffered the quickest pummeling ever dished out on a major league diamond.

No sooner had the Reds taken the field at Ebbets Field than a 15-run first-inning debacle was underway. Cincinnati forgot what an out was. During the shellacking in the first frame, the Dodgers sent 21 men to the plate. Everybody in the lineup hit safely except for Gil Hodges who walked twice. Before the third out was recorded, every player had scored and driven in at least one run. Nineteen men reached base safely on 10 hits, seven walks and two hit batsmen.

Nobody was more aware of just how ridiculous the inning was than Reds starting pitcher Ewell Blackwell. After manager Luke Sewell pulled him in the first inning and sent Bud Byerly in to relieve, Blackwell showered, changed into his street clothes and caught a cab back to the hotel. He went to the bar to watch the rest of the game on television. To his utter amazement, the game was still in the first inning. But Blackwell didn't share his embarrassment alone. Before the first inning was over, into the bar walked *his* reliever, Bud Byerly!

											R	H	E
CINCINNATI		0	0	0	0	1	0	0	0	0 —	1	5	0
BROOKLYN		(15)	0	2	0	2	0	0	0	x —	19	19	1

The Wrong Man

The Goats Who Got Away

OK, you history buffs. It's time to get a few things straightened out. For too many years, baseball has allowed some undeserving players to suffer untold abuse and ridicule for major blunders while the true villains have escaped scot-free. No more. Let's drag the real marbleheads out of hiding and give them the dishonor they deserve. For "The Goats Who Got Away," The Baseball Hall of SHAME inducts the following:

Hugh Casey
PITCHER · BROOKLYN, N.L. · OCT. 5, 1941

For decades now, Dodger catcher Mickey Owen has been scorned as one of baseball's biggest goats for dropping the infamous third strike that allowed the Yankees to win the crucial fourth game of the 1941 World Series.

He took the blame that rightfully belonged to pitcher Hugh Casey who threw a spitter only a backstop could have halted.

In the top of the ninth with the Dodgers leading 4–3, reliever Casey got the first two Yankees out and had worked the count on Tommy Henrich to 3–2. It looked like the Dodgers had locked up the game which would tie the Series at two wins apiece.

With the Ebbets Field crowd roaring, Casey threw a pitch that swerved erratically and completely fooled Henrich who swung and missed by a foot. He started for the dugout thinking the game was over. But the pitch also had fooled Owen. It bounced off the tip of his glove and careened to the backstop. Henrich raced to first.

Given new life, the Yankees Joe DiMaggio singled and Charlie Keller doubled off Casey. (Although Casey was obviously rattled, manager Leo Durocher didn't budge from the dugout nor call time to give the shaken pitcher time to calm down.) Casey then walked Bill Dickey and gave up another double to Joe Gordon. By the time Casey got the third out, the Yankees had scored four ninth-inning runs to win 7–4. The demoralized Dodgers went on to lose the Series, four games to one.

Forever after, Owen was blamed for missing the third strike. But it wasn't his fault. Casey threw an illegal spitter so wet Owen would have needed a raincoat and umbrella to catch it. Second of all, the catcher didn't know that the spitter was coming. Even if he had known, Owen, who in 128 games that season permitted only two passed balls, couldn't have caught that spitter with a hockey net.

So Hugh Casey really deserves the goat horns, especially since he reportedly admitted years later he had loaded up the fatal pitch.

Bucky Walters

PITCHER · CINCINNATI, N.L. · OCT. 8, 1939

The incident made the headlines and the history books as "Schnozz's Snooze!" and "Ernie's Swoon."

The sportswriters dumped all over Cincinnati Reds catcher Ernie Lombardi in one of the most unfair treatments any ballplayer has suffered at the hands of the press. If anyone deserved to be picked on, it should have been pitcher Bucky Walters in the final game of the 1939 World Series.

The Yankees had already pulverized the Reds in three straight games and were gunning for a Series sweep. The fourth game was tied 4–4 in the top of the tenth inning when the Yankees scored a run and had Charlie Keller on first. Joe DiMaggio then lined a hit to left. Outfielder Ival Goodman bobbled the ball and Keller tried to score from first.

The throw from the outfield came in low, bounced and caught Ernie in the worst place imaginable—right smack in the protective cup. Lombardi acted like any man would in that situation—he collapsed in agony. To make matters worse, Keller crashed into Lombardi at the plate. While Lombardi lay crumpled in a dazed heap, DiMaggio ran around the bases and also scored.

The Yankees won the game 7–4 and the Series. The press blamed Lombardi for suffering a mental lapse. That's like telling a wounded combat soldier he shouldn't have stepped in the path of a speeding bullet.

If there's a culprit, it's Bucky Walters who stayed on the mound and didn't back up the play at the plate as he should have. Had he done so, the Reds might have stopped DiMaggio from scoring. If anyone took a snooze it was Walters.

Rube Benton   Walter Holke
PITCHER   FIRST BASEMAN
NEW YORK, N.L. · OCT. 15, 1917

Nobody felt the pain and humiliation of the 1917 World Series more than Giant third baseman Heinie Zimmerman. He was the one who had to shoulder the blame of blowing the final game when in his heart he knew his teammates were the real goats.

The White Sox were leading the Series three games to two. The sixth and final game was scoreless until the fourth inning when Zimmerman's troubles began. With Chicago runners on first and third, batter Happy Felsch hit a high bouncer back to the mound. Pitcher Rube Benton, seeing runner Eddie Collins halfway between third and home, threw to Zimmerman.

Catcher Bill Rariden came up the line to start a rundown. But incredibly, Benton and first baseman Walter Holke looked like they had grown roots. Both forgot one of the fundamentals of baseball—cover home. Collins seized the opportunity and sprinted past Rariden for home. With nobody to throw to at home, Zimmerman had no choice but to chase the speedy Collins. Pawing frantically in the air with the ball, Zimmerman never had a prayer of catching Collins who scored.

It was the turning point of the game because the other runner and batter reached third and second, respectively, on the play. A single drove in both Sox runners and Chicago won 4–2, to capture the world championship.

The headlines screamed of "Zim's Boner," but the real blame belonged to Benton and Holke for not protecting home plate.

Hank O'Day
UMPIRE · SEPT. 23, 1908

Until the day he died, New York Giants infielder Fred Merkle had to wear the unfair label as the quintessential bonehead of baseball.

He was only 19 when his name turned to shame in a game against the Cubs who were battling the Giants in a tense pennant race. The teams had fought to a 1–1 tie but the Giants threatened in the bottom of the ninth inning.

With two out, the Giants had Moose McCormick on third and Merkle

George Brace Photo

on first. The next batter, Al Bridwell, lined a hit into center easily scoring McCormick with what should have been the winning run. But Merkle, seeing the run score, turned and headed for the clubhouse without touching second. Back then it was a common practice among veterans. Even though the rule said the runner had to touch the base, it was never enforced.

However, the Cubs Johnny Evers had been reading the rule book. He started yelling for the ball. A force out at second would nullify the run and the game would have to go on. As the relay came in, Giants pitcher Joe McGinnity realized what was happening. He ran out, wrestled the ball away from the relay man and hurled it into the stands. The Cubs retaliated by throwing a second ball out from the dugout. Evers touched second and appealed to umpire Hank O'Day who called Merkle out even though the out was made with an illegal ball in play. A near riot ensued and the game was called a tie.

The next day, Merkle was blasted unmercifully by the press. One account began: "Through the inexcusable stupidity of Merkle, a substitute, the Giants had a sure victory turned into a doubtful one, a game was played in dispute, a complicated and disagreeable controversy was started, and perhaps the championship imperiled or lost."

Despite protests to league officials, O'Day's ruling held. The game was replayed on the final day of the season with both teams sporting identical 98–55 records. The Cubs won 4–2 and claimed the pennant.

Within weeks after the incident, a depressed Merkle lost fifteen pounds and would have quit baseball if not for the sympathetic handling by his manager John McGraw.

As long as he lived, McGraw believed the Giants had been swindled out of the league championship. But he never blamed Merkle. "He did not cost us the pennant," the manager said. "We lost a dozen games we should have won, and any one of them could have saved the pennant for us."

Nevertheless, Merkle could never escape the taunts and jibes. Witless people who said goodbye to him often quipped, "So long, Fred. Don't forget to touch second."

Cruel remarks finally forced him out of the game that had so wronged him. His last job in organized baseball was managing the Class D Daytona-Ormand club in Florida. One day in 1929, Merkle walked off the field never to return again when a young player called him "bonehead."

Later, Merkle remarked with bitterness, "When I die, I guess they'll put on my tombstone, 'Here Lies Bonehead Merkle.'"

Razing the Roof

The Worst Ballparks for Watching and Playing Games

The unimaginative, circular, all-purpose stadiums now dominating the game are definitely drab and impersonal. They're nothing like the ballparks erected before domes, artificial turf, and theater seats. The old structures had style, color, and charm. Oh yeah? Some were built by people who must have hated baseball because inside these monstrosities fans and players alike have frozen and fried and risked life and limb. For "The Worst Ballparks for Watching and Playing Games," The Baseball Hall of SHAME inducts the following:

Candlestick Park
SAN FRANCISCO · 1960–PRESENT

Candlestick Park has been called everything except a stadium. "The Abomination by the Bay" and "Baseball's Alcatraz" are some of the kinder monikers.

Everybody suffers in Candlestick. Ask pitcher Stu Miller. He was charged with a balk after getting knocked off balance by a 60 m.p.h. gust during the 1961 All-Star Game—one which convinced the world that Candlestick might make a good experimental wind tunnel.

When the All-Star contest started, it was a hot and humid 81 degrees. As a result, 22 fans were carried out with heat exhaustion in the early innings. By the seventh frame, a cold, howling wind forced the bullpen pitchers to bundle up in blankets to keep warm.

Candlestick is the only outdoor stadium in the world that requires heating. Since the thermometer commonly plunges to 40 degrees or lower at night, the park was built with a radiant heat system to keep 20,000 of the choice seats nice and toasty. But that doesn't help the players any.

At Candlestick there is no such thing as a routine fly ball. For years, outfielders have been sandblasted by the gale force winds whipping off the bay. Infielders make bets on which county the popups will land. Once, Met third baseman Rod Kanehl raced back after a windblown pop fly behind third and then watched in amazement as it fell near *first* base. Typically, players spend more time chasing their caps than they do balls. Adding to their woes are the tricky hops off the infield caused by building the park on an abandoned landfill which is still settling.

Is it any wonder that in a 1983 poll, the National League ball players named Candlestick as the worst stadium in the league?

Municipal Stadium

CLEVELAND · 1932–PRESENT

The fans in Cleveland have been putting up with their "Mistake on the Lake" since major league baseball debuted there in 1932. And it doesn't look like the nightmare will go away any time soon.

When the American League players were asked to rate the stadiums they played in, there was no contest. Municipal Stadium was given "the pits" rating as the worst. The complaints throughout the league were nearly identical: "... terrible field conditions ... poor seating ... sewers backing up in the dugouts ..."

The fans were not asked for their opinions. It wouldn't have mattered. They're usually too frozen to reply anyway. Perched like a beached whale on the shore of chilly Lake Erie, the 70,000-plus seat structure was not built, as rumor has it, as the world's largest refrigerator.

The winter winds take their spring break in Cleveland. For early season night games, fans are bundled up warmer than dog sled racers. Their knees click like castanets from shivering. More than once ushers have been forced to put out little camp fires in the stands when fans tried to keep warm.

Los Angeles Coliseum

LOS ANGELES · 1958–61

When Walter O'Malley brought his Dodgers into town in 1958, he picked the 102,000-seat Coliseum as his temporary stadium. Never mind that it was built for the Olympics and not for baseball; that the playing area could not properly accommodate a major league field; or that it was brutally hot for fans and players during the summer.

The Coliseum was nothing more than a giant kiln, so hot you could glaze pottery inside it. The first weekend the Dodgers played there the fans looked like victims of a forced march across the Sahara, dropping like flies from the 100-degree heat.

The fans who weren't sizzling in their shadeless seats—actually the seats were straight-backed benches harder than church pews—were gasping for breath as they struggled to the top of its 65 rows. From way up there no one could be sure just what those little bitty fellows were doing down there on the Coliseum floor.

Baseball belonged in the Coliseum about as much as a punk rock concert in Sun City. The stadium's dimensions were the bad joke of the National League—425 feet to center and 440 feet to distant right. Players cut years off their careers just walking to and from their positions.

But the real monstrosity was the left field fence, the infamous Chinese Screen. In order to shoehorn even the semblance of a diamond into the Coliseum, the left field fence was only 251 feet from home plate. The

Dodgers had to erect a 42-foot-high screen that extended 140 feet out towards center field from the left field foul line. Over this contraption they draped a bunch of chicken wire. Power sluggers' booming line drives that normally would go for 400-foot homers in other parks bounced off the Chinese Screen for measly singles. But Little League popups from banjo hitters dropped behind the screen for homers. The screen infuriated baseball purists and for a while there was even talk of disallowing any home runs hit over it. They should have disallowed baseball playing altogether in the Coliseum.

Baker Bowl

PHILADELPHIA · 1883–1938

The old barn at Broad and Huntington was a killer. Literally. Twice sections of the delapidated stands collapsed causing the death of 13 fans and injuries to hundreds of others.

In their own way, pitchers died a thousand times watching home run after home run disappear over the ridiculously short 272-foot right field fence.

Baker Bowl, which held only 20,000 spectators, sported some of the oddest features ever incorporated into a ballpark's design. There was a swimming pool in an area behind the center field fence and an embanked 15-foot-wide bicycle track rimming the outfield where players ran up and down its incline chasing fly balls.

Depending on how you look at it, those were the niceties. The facilities for the players, on the other hand, had a lot in common with the Black Hole of Calcutta. A writer at the time once noted: "National League players will be pleased to learn that the visiting dressing room at Baker Bowl is being completely refurbished for next season—brand new nails are being installed on which to hang their clothes."

But the laughing stopped on Aug. 6, 1903. A fight broke out on 15th Street behind the left field stands and when about 500 spectators rushed to the back railing to watch the action, the rotten joists gave way and the balcony plunged to the street. Twelve people were killed and over 200 injured.

Somebody should have gotten the message from the tragedy that Baker Bowl was dangerous. They didn't and it happened again when the Phillies were playing the Cardinals on May 14, 1927. An entire section of the right field stands fell like a house of cards. Thousands of spectators tumbled on top of the unfortunates at the bottom of the pile. Hundreds poured out onto the diamond in panic. Scores were injured and one person was trampled to death.

There should have been a condemnation order issued on the spot, but incredibly Baker Bowl was patched together once more and carried on as baseball's slum for another decade until it was demolished and sold for scrap.

Colt Stadium

HOUSTON · 1962–64

There was one good thing to be said about the first home of the expansion team Colt 45s (later renamed Astros). It didn't last long. If it had, it might have been the end of Houston baseball for a very basic reason. Neither players nor fans could have long survived its tortures—unbearable heat, poor lighting and, worst of all, mosquitoes.

Colt Stadium's singular claim to fame is that it was the only park in history where the concession stands sold more mosquito repellent than beer. Women spectators didn't wear perfume, they wore "Off!" Everything is always bigger in Texas and that includes mosquitoes, gnats, and horseflies. In fact, the term infield fly took on a whole new meaning in Houston.

Fans foolish enough to attend a game sweltered and steamed in the oppressive heat. That simmering humidity coming off the nearby smelly swamp sent 100 spectators to the first aid station during one Sunday afternoon double-header.

However bad it was for the fans in the stands it was worse for the players on the field.

Determined to keep their hold on their swampland, the swarms of twin-engine mosquitoes and bugs gave the visiting ball players more competition than the Colt 45s.

Players also risked career-ending injuries during night games because the park was so dimly lighted. When he was a Met in 1962, Richie Ashburn complained, "If they're going to play night ball there, at least they should put in lights."

Yer Out, Ump!

Umpires Who Were Banished, Suspended or Fined

Umpires are a special breed of tyrant. The men in blue are powerful, iron-fisted rulers on the field, controlling the fate of the players with a flick of the wrist or the utterance of a word. But, as is proven in history, power tends to corrupt. And it's no different in baseball. For "Umpires Who Were Banished, Suspended or Fined," The Baseball Hall of SHAME inducts the following:

Richard Higham
1882

Richard Higham has the distinction of being the only umpire ever booted out of baseball for his blatant dishonesty.

He should have been kicked out just as much for the stupid way he set up his bumbling scam as for his cheating.

Before he turned to umpiring, Higham had been benched as a player in Chicago for his highly suspicious inept play in losses by the White Stockings, so his shady calls as a man in blue came as no great surprise.

The first to smell something fishy was William Thompson, the mayor of Detroit and the president of the local ball club then called the Wolverines. He noticed that Higham, who umpired 26 out of the first 29 Wolverine games at the start of the 1882 season, almost always made close calls against Detroit. So Thompson hired a private detective to investigate

Higham. The gumshoe turned up a letter that Higham had mailed to a well known gambler of the day in which he outlined a childishly simple code on how and when to bet. If, for example, Higham wanted the bets put down on Detroit to win, he would signal the gambler by telegram to "Buy all the lumber you can." If the gambler received no telegram he was to bet on Detroit's opponent.

Armed with that evidence, Thompson and the other owners confronted the crooked ump and he was banished from the game. Higham went back to Chicago and took up a profession more suited to his ilk. He became a bookmaker.

Tim Hurst

1891–1909

The terrible-tempered Timothy Hurst had rather unorthodox ways of settling arguments with players who disputed his calls. He either punched them in the face or spat in their eye.

To their dismay and pain, many players discovered Hurst's favorite way of proving the umpire is always right—he clobbered them over the head with his mask. If Hurst felt the insult too great and the punishment too minor, he would track down the offending player at his hotel after the game and thrash him some more.

Hurst's pugnacious behavior was so bad he was thrown out of the National League. He came back to umpire in the American League a few years later and made it a clean sweep by getting the heave-ho there too.

His ejection from the senior circuit followed an incident in Cincinnati on Aug. 4, 1897. To express displeasure over the way Hurst was calling the game, a fan tossed a beer stein out of the stands and hit the ump in the back. Hurst calmly picked it up and hurled it back. But the flying stein hit the wrong person in the face and knocked him cold. The fans exploded out onto the field in retaliation. All by himself, Hurst managed to fight them off until the cops escorted him from the field. For his action, Hurst was fined $100 and fired by National League officials.

Next, in a strange move that only the equally strange owner of the St. Louis Browns, Chris von der Ahe, could contemplate, Hurst was hired to manage the Browns. Hurst then went into his Jekyll and Hyde routine. From the most hated umpire in the game, he went to the most hated umpire-baiter in the game. His rousing battles with his former colleagues shook the grandstands wherever the Browns played. By the end of the season he had managed St. Louis to last place in the 12-team league and was fired.

By 1905, with the American League firmly established, he returned to baseball and brought with him the cantankerous, hostile Hurst style of umpiring.

Sometimes he fought over his fancy patent leather pumps that he wore on the field. Managers had a way of standing extra close to make a point about a bad call. After one such confrontation, New York's manager, Clark Griffith, left a lot of untidy spike marks all over Hurst's tidy toes. The ump called time out, followed Griffith to the dugout and knocked him out with one punch.

On Aug. 4, 1909, twelve years to the day of the incident that banished him from the National League, Hurst triggered a fracas that led to his expulsion in the American League. Eddie Collins, the highly popular, college-bred second baseman for Philadelphia, questioned one of Hurst's decisions. "Get away from me or I'll spit in your eye!" Hurst threatened. Collins stood his ground and Hurst kept his promise. The riot that followed was merely a replay of the 1897 brawl that the ump had instigated in Cincinnati. The results were also the same. He was kicked out of baseball for the second time.

Hurst's only explanation for spitting in Collin's eye: "I just don't like college boys!"

George Magerkurth

1929–47

George Magerkurth turned to umpiring when he couldn't make it as a ball player. And from then on, he took out his frustration on every player who crossed his path.

The burly, six-foot, three-inch, 225-pound Magerkurth had learned to use his fists in 70 professional boxing matches. He relied on that experience to bully and intimidate anyone who dared question his calls. Magerkurth never seemed to know where the ring ended and the diamond began.

Although he commanded a reputation for unflinching honesty, his fights with players and spectators cost him several fines and suspensions. When he was calling balls and strikes in the American Association, he got into a dispute with Ivy Griffin, Milwaukee's promising first baseman. Still seething after the game, Magerkurth attacked Griffin in his hotel. Griffin's shoulder was dislocated in the fight and his career ended. Magerkurth was fined $25, suspended for 30 days, and then fired.

Nevertheless, the belligerent Magerkurth managed to get hired by the National League. One of his most notorious run-ins was with the Giants' star shortstop, Billy Jurges, during a melee at the Polo Grounds in July,

1939. With the Giants 'eading 4–3, plate umpire Lee Ballanfant called a drive along the left field foul line a fair ball. The ruling gave the Cincinnati Reds a 5–4 advantage ind infuriated the Giants. The dispute quickly escalated into a shoving match.

Magerkurth and Jurges ended up nose to nose shouting invectives in one another's face. Magerkurth chewed tobacco and tended to sputter when he was upset. The argument moved from baseball to spit when Jurges complained about the brown shower he was getting from the umpire.

"Take your ugly puss out of my face and I won't be spitting in it," Magerkurth shouted.

"Yeah, and I'll spit right in your ugly puss," Billy yelled back.

Magerkurth dared him to just try. Jurges spit a glob in the umpire's eye and the fight was on. When the dust had cleared Jurges was fined and suspended for spitting. Magerkurth drew a 10-day suspension and a $150 fine.

On July 19, 1945, Magerkurth beat up a fan in retaliation for a heckling he was getting in Cincinnati. The assault was ugly enough, but Magerkurth made it worse by punching the wrong person.

The victim, Thomas J. Longo, a Dayton restaurant owner, later explained that people near where he was seated in the front row during a Reds-Braves double-header had been giving Magerkurth a hard time. When the game ended, Magerkurth, his face red with anger, rushed to the railing and started berating Longo for calling him a "thief." Longo denied it and another fan sitting nearby took credit for the remark. Magerkurth didn't buy it. As Longo draped his coat over his arm and stood to leave, the angry umpire socked him in the eye. Longo filed assault charges that were later dropped when Magerkurth wrote a letter of apology and paid $100 for the victim's medical expenses.

Sleaze Plays

The Most Disgusting Role Models for America's Youth

Some players have been great role models—for boys in reform school. These players are the true foul balls whose exploits read better on a police blotter or porno house marquee than on the sports page. For "The Most Disgusting Role Models for America's Youth," The Baseball Hall of SHAME inducts the following:

Denny McLain

PITCHER · DETROIT-WASHINGTON, A.L. · 1963–72

Denny McLain stood on top of the world, but rather than enjoy the view, he carelessly fell into the pits of depravity.

Perhaps no baseball star had more going for him than Denny McLain. In 1968 he was named the American League's MVP after winning a remarkable 31 games. The following year he won 24 games, earning back-to-back Cy Young Awards.

Yet by 1970, at the age of twenty-six, McLain chose to self-destruct. That year he was on Commissioner Bowie Kuhn's carpet more often than the cleaning lady. He was suspended 132 days for gambling and consorting with bookmakers. Then he drew another suspension of thirty-eight days when he was caught packing a gun.

Throughout the year he complained loudly about the bad press he was getting. His unique approach to improving press relations was to dump buckets of ice water on two sportswriters. For that prank he was slapped with his third suspension of the year, this time for seven days. Adding to his woes, McLain, who was earning over $200,000 a year from baseball and endorsements, filed for bankruptcy.

Even before the 1970 season, McLain showed evidence that he was capable of losing everything his athletic ability had given him. In 1967, for instance, during a tight pennant race he sat in the dugout and explained to sportswriters why the Tigers would never make it to the World Series.

In 1969 he displayed an arrogance that disgusted all fans. When the All-Star Game was postponed one day by rain, he told everyone, "I've got an appointment to get my teeth capped and I'm not going to change it." Even though he was the scheduled starter, he hopped into his private plane, flew back to Detroit and had the dental work done on schedule. Denny showed up at the All-Star Game but not early enough to start.

The Detroit front office, fed up with his escapades and sickening 3–5 record in 1970, palmed him off to Washington. He lost 22 games for the Senators, thus descending in three years from the most games won in the majors to the most games lost—a dramatic plunge that may never be equalled. A year later he was out of baseball.

Ross Grimsley

PITCHER · CINCINNATI-MONTREAL, N.L.
BALTIMORE-CLEVELAND, A.L. · 1971–80

Ross Grimsley should have put a "G" in front of his first name. He went months wearing the same rank-smelling sweatshirt. And because of his bizarre superstition, he wouldn't wash, comb his hair or use deodorant when he was winning (thus causing teammates to consider throwing games when he pitched). He also shuffled around town shirtless in torn jeans and sandals—a sight that horrified mothers hid from their children.

A teammate once described Grimsley as the "most nauseating thing you've ever seen on two legs." That's why Grimsley earned the nickname "Skuz." He took great pride in his reputation as a pigpen who could pitch. One of his joys was his personal collection of sleazy photos. Fans sent him pictures of disgusting-looking people like bearded ladies and wolfmen with "Grimsley's sister" or "Grimsley's brother" written on them.

He gave his fans more of himself than most players. Once when a carload of young women followed the team bus, Grimsley showed his (cl)ass by shooting them a moon out of the rear window.

Grimsley claimed he was just out to have a good time. Once in a hotel, after he and a friend were tanked up, they shed their clothes and ran up to the roof. "We started swinging from the hotel sign like gorillas," he reported later. "One slip and we'd have gone splat, 20 floors down. But let me tell you, we wouldn't have felt it."

Babe Ruth

OUTFIELDER · BOSTON-NEW YORK, A.L. · BOSTON, N.L. · 1914–35

Thank goodness children never knew the real Babe Ruth. Imagine if they had. Millions of youngsters would have emulated their hero and indulged, like he did daily, in booze, buffets, and bimbos.

Babe carried on a naughty, decadent life without the public's knowledge because he had the New York press corps wrapped around his fat pinky. If the same reporters who hid the truth about Babe had been covering Ivan the Terrible, he would have gone down in history as a saint.

With the Babe, insiders looked the other way. Otherwise, he would have been up on morals charges more times than at bat. He was, for example, a gold medalist in the sexual olympics. He didn't consider the day complete without at least one romp with a nympho or whore. His glandular prowess reached legendary status during one road trip to St. Louis when he took on an entire brothel and sampled one hooker after another. He had more contact with V.D. than he did with curve balls.

Booze was another of his passions. He drank enough to flood Yankee Stadium. His breakfast juice consisted of a quart mixture of whiskey and ginger ale.

The Babe never met a meal he didn't like, but he outdid himself on the train trip home from spring training in 1925, suffering the biggest belly ache in baseball history. He had gorged himself on yards of hot dogs and gallons of ice cream which were washed down by beer and liquor. By the time the train to New York had reached Asheville, North Carolina, Ruth was doubled over in pain. An ambulance met the train and rushed the slugger to the nearest hospital where he was treated for acute indigestion. (Some sources swear the real reason he was hospitalized was because he suffered a severe case of venereal disease.)

Because of his hospitalization and recuperation, Ruth was out of the lineup for several weeks. When he returned, he played in only 98 games, hit nearly 50 points below his lifetime average and had only 25 home runs. Without his constant, game-winning power, the Yankees finished seventh.

It was a bad year for Ruth in other ways. On road trips, he was constantly breaking training rules, carousing until the wee hours of the morning. Yankee manager Miller Huggins was so furious at Babe's debauchery that he fined Ruth $5,000. The fine didn't hurt Babe all that much—not to a man who dropped enormous sums of cash at the race track.

On the field, Ruth was hardly the team player. Although he and Lou Gehrig were always pictured together smiling with their arms around each other, the truth was that Babe had little use for Gehrig because Lou had refused to hold out with him for more money during contract negotiations.

As a result, Babe went long stretches without speaking to Lou. But at least Ruth knew who Gehrig was. Babe didn't even bother to learn the names of many of his teammates. Introduced to one player who'd been on the roster for two years, Ruth thought the player was a rookie.

But Babe made sure his teammates knew he was the highest paid player in baseball. He liked to wave his paycheck under their noses and taunt them about how much he was getting compared to them.

His image as the grinning, moon-faced, big-hearted lug who promised home runs to dying little boys was tarnished by his meanness. In 1922, while arguing over an out call by umpire George Hildebrand during a game, Ruth threw a handful of dirt in the arbiter's face. Naturally, Ruth was thrown out of the game. As Babe headed for the dugout still shouting and cursing, a fan in the stands razzed him. Grabbing a bat, Ruth climbed over the dugout roof and chased the much smaller fan out of the stadium.

American League President Ban Johnson decided not to suspend Ruth. But he fined him $200 for throwing dirt at the ump and ordered Babe to give up his honorary title of captain of the Yankees. Johnson said Ruth was "tempermentally unfit" to serve in that capacity.

Babe was crushed. He had lusted after the title and had bullied the Yankees into giving it to him. He was captain for only six days.

That same year Ruth was at his worst and drew five different suspensions, usually for abusive language to umpires. In a letter to Babe, Ban Johnson read him the riot act: "It seems the period has arrived when you should allow some intelligence to creep into a mind that has plainly been warped."

Albert "Sparky" Lyle

PITCHER · BOSTON-NEW YORK-TEXAS, A.L. · PHILADELPHIA, N.L.
1967–82

Sparky made the most bizarre impressions on the game—by sitting bare-assed on birthday cakes.

Sparky began his epic streak when he was with the Red Sox. Teammate Ken Harrelson's birthday cake, a kelly-green replica of Fenway Park, had been delivered to the locker room. In one of those flashes of historic inspiration, Sparky planted his bare behind on the gooey miniature Fenway. From then on, whenever a birthday cake appeared, so did Albert Wayne Lyle, derriere at the ready.

When Sparky went to the Yankees, he took his unbroken cake-sitting streak with him. Within two weeks, the unsuspecting Yankees had someone's birthday cake delivered to the clubhouse. Sensing pinstripe immortality, Sparky seized the opportunity to display to his awed teammates his championship squatting form. The cake happened to be for manager Ralph Houk who suddenly lost his appetite.

Ted Williams

OUTFIELDER · BOSTON, A.L. · 1939–60

Ted Williams could have held the respect of players and fans alike, but he threw it away like a wild-armed fielder.

Ted's reputation as a lout was a result of his career-long churlish behavior that included spitting at the stands, obscene gestures to fans, and displays of childish pouting on the field.

One of his worst offenses came following a strikeout. In a fit of anger, Ted hurled his bat toward the stands where it struck a woman on the head.

He often treated the Boston fans, who supported him for so many years, with utter contempt. In 1950 during the first game of a double-header with Detroit, he dropped an easy fly ball that sparked a howl from the boo birds. In response, Williams stuck his thumbs in his ears and wiggled his fingers in a braying jackass gesture. In the second game, the

Tigers had loaded the bases when Vic Wertz hit a ball to left that bounced past Ted to the wall. Instead of hustling to hold the base runners, Williams leisurely trotted after the ball, picked it up and studied it for a moment before tossing it back toward the infield as Wertz slid safely into third. Ted's lackadaisical play set off the howls again. When the inning ended, Ted leaped into the air and delivered the classic one-finger salute to the booing crowd. Then, just to make sure there was no misunderstanding, he turned to his left and then to his right and repeated the obscene gesture for the benefit of those in the bleachers.

On July 20, 1956, Joe Cronin, the Red Sox general manager and former star shortstop, was being honored in Fenway for his election into the Hall of Fame. It was also the night Ted hit his 400th home run—and discovered spit. By now his feud with the Boston fans and sportswriters was an institution at Fenway. As Williams crossed the plate after hitting the historic homer, he showed his contempt by spitting toward the writers in the press box.

A few weeks later, on August 7, he sprayed the park again. In a home game against the Yankees, Williams mishandled a fly ball in the eleventh inning. Fans jeered him as he came in from the outfield and Ted began spitting back at them as he neared the Red Sox dugout. That did it. Cronin levied a $5,000 fine against Williams. "We just can't condone that sort of thing," Cronin declared.

Williams' response was typical: "I'm not a bit sorry for what I did. I'd spit again at the same fans who booed me today."

Free Agent Flops

The Most Ridiculous Free Agent Signings

Did somebody call them FREE agents? Who do they think they're kidding? There's nothing free about those high salaries and bizarre bonus clauses for mediocre players. Ever since the free agent signings in 1976, the owners have paid millions for damaged goods and players whose talents are worth no more than bus tickets home. Some of these free agents are out of baseball before the ink is even dry on their gilt-edged contracts. Others get rich just sitting on the bench. For "The Most Ridiculous Free Agent Signings," The Baseball Hall of SHAME inducts the following:

Andy Messersmith
PITCHER · ATLANTA, N.L. · APRIL 10, 1976

The pioneer of modern-day free agency was also the system's first flop.

Messersmith had pitched for the Dodgers less often than he pouted over his contract. He wanted out, so he sued and won. With the reserve clause now worthless, Messersmith, a 19-game winner, went out shopping for another team.

He found a sucker in Georgia and dug right into Braves owner Ted Turner's deep pockets to the tune of $1.75 million for three years. The salary was big money for its time and triggered runaway salary offers for other free agents.

The Braves paid dearly for what they got. Messersmith faded faster than a spitter down and away. After an injury, he won 16 and lost 15 in two years of service.

Fortunately for Turner, he found a fellow sucker. Turner peddled Messersmith to New York where George Steinbrenner paid $100,000 to learn that the pitcher was useless. The Yankees cut him loose after the injury-prone hurler failed to win a game for them. By 1979 he was out of baseball.

Ron Blomberg

OUTFIELDER · CHICAGO, A.L. · NOV. 17, 1977

When the free agent price wars were heating up, White Sox owner Bill Veeck voiced his criticism over owners who sign players of uncertain ability for big-buck, long-term contracts.

To prove his point about this idiocy, Veeck then gave former Yankee Ron Blomberg a four-year, $600,000 contract—even though Blomberg had been almost totally incapacitated with knee and shoulder injuries for the previous three years, hitting only .255 in just 35 games during that period. In fact, he was on the disabled list for all of 1977.

When he was wheeled into Comiskey Park, Blomberg quickly demonstrated he had more business being in a rehabilitation center than on a ball field. Blomberg played in 61 games in 1978, hit only .231 with 5 homers and 22 RBIs. Veeck had seen enough and so had the fans. Blomberg was released.

Rennie Stennett

SECOND BASEMAN · SAN FRANCISCO, N.L. · DEC. 12, 1979

Everybody in baseball knew that Rennie Stennett couldn't move the same since he broke his ankle in 1977. Everybody, that is, except the Giants front office. Maybe nobody read the sports pages to them.

Whatever the reason, after the 1979 season, the Giants begged Stennett, who hit .238 that year, to accept $3 million for the next five years. Nobody can blame Stennett for taking found money from a Sugar Daddy. The front office, though, did wonder why it was so easy signing up Stennett. There was really no mystery. No one else was bidding for his services.

The Giants were surprised in 1980 when Stennett struggled at the plate and hit only .244. He rode the bench most of 1981 before he was sent packing in 1982 while the Giants choked on the $2 million they still had to pay him.

Dave Goltz

PITCHER · LOS ANGELES, N.L. · NOV. 14, 1979

Dodger management let star pitcher Tommy John get away and then shelled out $3 million for ex-Twin hurler Dave Goltz in a six-year pact. The eight previous years with Minnesota, Goltz had a 96–79 record. But that was history. The Dodgers got far less than they bargained for. In 1980, Goltz won only seven games, lost 11 and had a lackluster ERA of 4.32. The next year he pitched even worse, losing eight of ten decisions. After that, the Dodgers ate the rest of his contract.

Don Stanhouse

PITCHER · LOS ANGELES, N.L. · NOV. 17, 1979

Don Stanhouse rode west out of the Baltimore bullpen and, without even using a mask, robbed the Dodgers of $2.1 million. He was Los Angeles' second free agency shot in the dark in 1979 and once again the team bigwigs misfired. The question is why did the Dodgers want him anyway? Stanhouse had a lifetime mark of 36–51 before he joined the team.

In his one year with the Dodgers, Stanhouse recorded two wins, two losses and a fat 5.04 ERA. It took the Dodgers even less time to dine on Stanhouse's contract than on Goltz's.

Wayne Garland

PITCHER · CLEVELAND, A.L. · NOV. 19, 1976

In their rush to make Wayne Garland a wealthy man, the Indians pulled off one of the worst free agency deals on record.

They signed the former Oriole, who had won a total of only 27 games in the previous three years, to a 10-year, $2.3 million contract. His first year in Cleveland, Garland never lived up to his potential or salary. He had five straight losing seasons with Cleveland and was cut loose in 1982 after sporting a poor 28–48 record with the team.

Al Hrabosky

PITCHER · ATLANTA, N.L. · NOV. 20, 1979

Al Hrabosky became the highest-paid, least-worked relief pitcher in baseball.

Hrabosky, who had never pitched 100 innings in any one season, signed with the Braves to pitch for five years. But under the terms of the contract, owner Ted Turner agreed to keep the man with the Fu Manchu mustache on the payroll for the next 35 years. Moreover, Turner promised to find Hrabosky a slot in his broadcasting empire when the pitcher's career was over—which was much sooner than Turner expected.

For his part, Hrabosky agreed to come out of the bullpen when he could find the time and more or less pitch a few innings in relief. It was a lot less than more.

With his $5.9 million contract, partly deferred at 10 percent interest to be paid over the 35-year period at the rate of about $170,000 annually and his $250,000 signing bonus and his no-trade clause through the 1982 season, Hrabosky developed a sore arm. His salary was more impressive than his pitching.

During his three seasons with the Braves, Hrabosky had the grand total of seven wins and four losses. In 1981, he was used primarily for one-out appearances against left-handed hitters. His record was 1–1 with a single save. When he was released by the Braves in 1982, he asked if he could just hang around the bullpen. And there he sat, a monument to free agency craziness.

Run for your Lives!

The Most Outrageous Base-Running Fiascos

Some players are such horrendous runners they could use a second base coach. It's not that their legs are slow so much as it is their minds are working at only quarter speed. To others, running the base paths can be as reckless and foolish as strolling down a dark alley at midnight. For "The Most Outrageous Base-Running Fiascos," The Baseball Hall of SHAME inducts the following:

John Anderson

OUTFIELDER · WASHINGTON, A.L. · 1905

John Anderson is the spiritual leader of base-running blunderers. Anderson pulled such a dunderheaded move that for years afterward, any boner in or out of baseball was ridiculed as a "John Anderson."

Ironically, Anderson was known as a hustler who made things happen with his daring base running and dynamic batting. He was the spark that could ignite a team and turn certain defeat into glorious triumph.

But his glittering reputation was forever tainted by one unforgettable moment. With two out in the ninth inning and trailing by a run, the Senators had loaded the bases. Anderson was the runner on first.

George Brace Photo

It was in moments like this that great players made their mark in history. Anderson made his—a skid mark into ignominy.

Anderson edged off first base as the pitcher looked in for the sign. Suddenly, John took off on a mad dash for second. Only after he slid into second base did he realize that it was occupied. John Anderson was called out, ending the game. He had pulled off the first "John Anderson."

Babe Ruth

OUTFIELDER · NEW YORK, A.L. · OCT. 10, 1926

The Babe pulled the biggest boneheaded play of his career. And it cost the Yankees their last shot at the 1926 world championship.

In the top of the ninth inning of the seventh and final game of the World Series, the Cardinals were ahead 3–2. It is at historic moments like this that great heroes emerge. Or great goats are born. This happened to be the day of the goat. And its name was Ruth.

Cardinals relief pitcher Grover Cleveland Alexander managed to get the first two Yankees out. Then Ruth drew a walk and cleanup hitter Bob Meusel strode to the plate with Lou Gehrig on deck.

At this point, even a rookie would have known enough not to risk the third out by trying to steal. But Ruth was no rookie. Instead, without receiving any signal to steal, the overweight Ruth, who had stolen only 11 bases the entire season, took off for second with all the speed of a sedated elephant.

Catcher Bob O'Farrell was frozen in open-mouthed amazement as Ruth lumbered toward second, but the catcher recovered in plenty of time to make the throw to Rogers Hornsby, who easily tagged Ruth out by a good ten feet. Third out. End of game. End of Series.

"He didn't say a word," Hornsby recalled. "He didn't even look at me. He just picked himself up off the ground and walked away."

Lamented Yankee executive Ed Barrow: "It was Ruth's only dumb play of his life."

Marv Throneberry

FIRST BASEMAN · NEW YORK, N.L. · JUNE 17, 1962

Marvelous Marv Thoneberry endeared himself to Met fans with his atrocious fielding. But on this day, he showed the world that his base-running skills were just as awful.

In a game against the Chicago Cubs at the Polo Grounds, Throneberry whacked a triple to the right field bullpen. Head down, he chugged around first. Gathering all the steam of a hamstrung moose, Throneberry passed second and rambled to third. There he stood, huffing and puffing, reveling in the cheers from the fans who rarely saw Throneberry run the bases. Stumble over them, yes, but seldom run them.

As the applause began to fade, Cubs first baseman Ernie Banks strolled over to umpire Dusty Boggess. "Didn't touch first, you know," Banks said.

George Brace Photo

He called for the ball and calmly stepped on first. Boggess called Throneberry out.

Met manager Casey Stengel stormed out of the dugout to protest. A Met coach stopped him at the third base line. "Don't bother, Case," the coach said. "He missed second too."

Jimmy St. Vrain

PITCHER · CHICAGO, N.L. · 1902

Jimmy St. Vrain lasted only 12 games in the majors, but not before leaving a legacy of base-running stupidity.

St. Vrain had a problem finding first base. This is understandable since he seldom made it to first, batting a weak .097 for the year.

A lefty on the mound, St. Vrain usually batted right-handed but could seldom connect the bat with the ball. In a moment of pity, Cub manager Frank Selee suggested St. Vrain try batting left-handed.

Wonder of wonders, on his very next trip to the plate against the Pittsburgh Pirates, St. Vrain hit the ball. OK, so it only went as far as Honus Wagner at shortstop. That mattered not to the thrilled St. Vrain. He had hit the ball. In his excitement, he dropped the bat and took off on a dead run— toward third base!

For a moment, Wagner stood holding the ball in stunned amazement watching wrong-way St. Vrain race up the third base line. Wagner didn't know where to throw the ball. To first for the out or to third for the tag? He recovered in time and fired to first. It was probably the first time a runner was thrown out by 180 feet.

Babe Herman   Chick Fewster

FIRST BASEMAN   SECOND BASEMAN

Dazzy Vance

PITCHER
BROOKLYN, N.L. · AUG. 15, 1926

This was an immortal day in baseball history. Three Dodger runners decided to hold a meeting on third base during a game. Actually, Babe Herman, one of the daffiest of the "Daffiness Boys," had hit a double that turned into a double play.

It happened in the seventh inning of a 1–1 tie in a game against the Boston Braves. With one out, the Dodgers had loaded the bases—Hank DeBerry on third, Vance on second, and Fewster on first. That brought up

Herman who lined a hard shot to right for a sure double, maybe a triple.

DeBerry scored. Vance, who normally was about as fast as molasses in winter, held up until he saw the ball carom off the wall. He then headed for third with Fewster right on his heels. And behind them both, rounding second, came the galloping Herman, head down, arms pumping.

Coach Mickey O'Neill saw trouble brewing so he yelled at Herman, "Back! Back!" Vance thought the coach was talking to him so he hustled back to third base just in time to meet Fewster arriving from second. Then Herman came sliding in and found himself hugging not only the bag but Fewster and Vance as well.

Disgusted with the whole mess. Fewster walked off toward the dugout, figuring he was already out. By now the relay had reached third baseman Eddie Taylor, who, confused as the rest, proceeded to tag everyone in the neighborhood. To make sure the right guy was out, second baseman Doc Gautreau then grabbed the ball, chased down Fewster and tagged him too.

When it was finally all sorted out, the umpires ruled that Vance was safe at third since he got there first. Fewster was tagged out and Herman was called out for passing Fewster on the basepath.

Sighed beleaguered Dodger manager Wilbert Robinson. "That's the first time those guys got together on anything all season."

Grounds for Complaint

The Most Blatant Cases of Skulduggery by Groundskeepers

If you look carefully at the playing field, you can spot the sneaky handiwork of the devious doctors of dirt. A little sand here, a lot of water there on the base paths can slow down the fastest runner. Growing the grass higher between third and home can keep an aging infielder in the lineup longer. In any other sport this would be called cheating. In baseball, it's called groundskeeping. For "The Most Blatant Cases of Skulduggery by Groundskeepers," The Baseball Hall of SHAME inducts the following:

Baltimore Orioles Groundskeepers

AUG. 13, 1978

The Orioles beat the Yankees 3–0, in Memorial Stadium on a masterful late inning relief performance by the Baltimore groundskeepers.

In the top of the seventh inning of a rain-soaked game, the Orioles lost a 3–0 lead as the Yankees exploded for five runs. Before Baltimore could bat in the bottom half of the inning, heavy rains drenched the field, forcing a delay.

Normally, when given the word, the grounds crew will rush onto the field and spread the tarpaulin in record time to save the infield from soaking.

But the Baltimore crew was in no rush. Ever so slowly, they wandered out onto the field. Rain that had collected on the tarp was dumped onto the already soggy area in left field rather than onto foul territory as was customary. Taking their sweet time, the crew ploddingly dragged the tarp over the infield. By the time they finished the job, they all could have collected Social Security.

By then it didn't matter that they had established a new standard for pokiness. The playing field was only slightly drier than Johnstown during the great flood.

The game had to be called. Since the Orioles didn't get to bat in the last of the seventh, the score reverted back to the last complete inning. Thus, the Orioles won 3–0. Credit the save to the grounds crew.

San Francisco Giants Groundskeepers
1962

Every team in the league tried every trick in the book to slow down Maury Wills in his dash for base stealing glory in 1962. But nobody was as blatantly underhanded about it as the Giants grounds crew.

Whenever the Dodgers came to Candlestick Park, they found a soggy bog where first base used to be. The base path between first and second was so soaked that the Dodgers dubbed Marty Schwab, the Giants' chief groundskeeper, "Swampy" for his handiwork with the hose.

The area was so damp during one game that umpire Tom Gorman held up play for an hour and a half so the base path would dry out at least to the point that Wills didn't sink out of sight. If it wasn't water it was sand. One day there was so much sand dumped between first and second that it looked like the Giants had imported a beach. Maury, who swiped 104 bases that year, protested and the umpires delayed the game until the sand had been scooped up and trucked away.

Philadelphia Phillies Groundskeepers
1955

Even though the groundskeepers weren't on the Phillies roster, Richie Ashburn considered them "teammates." They helped him win the batting title in 1955.

Ashburn was adept at dropping bunts down the third base line and beating out the throw to first. In any other ball park, the odds were 50–50 that a bunt on the line would go fair or foul. But in the Phils home park, Connie Mack Stadium, the odds were improved considerably with a little bit of gardening that came to be known as "Ashburn's Ridge."

With some expert sculpting by the groundskeepers, the third base foul line was inclined and sloped toward the infield. A ball needed diesel power to get up and over that ridge into foul territory. By the time a bunt rolled dead in fair territory, Ashburn usually was safe on first. The first thing rival managers did when arriving in Philly was to stomp up and down on the Ashburn Ridge trying to flatten out the advantage. Their efforts did little to alter the finely crafted slope.

Ashburn took the batting title with a .338 average—thanks in part to the Ashburn Ridge.

Washington Senators Groundskeepers

AUG. 15, 1941

The Washington groundskeepers performed a disappearing act that they thought would win the game for the home team. Instead it cost the Senators a victory.

Washington was beating Boston 6–3 when it started pouring rain in the seventh inning. The umpires called time, sent the teams to the clubhouse and ordered that the field be covered. They waited a few minutes but nothing happened. Again, the order was given to cover the field. But there was no one to drag out the tarp.

The Washington grounds crew, usually so vigilant and trustworthy, had vanished. Even the Senators management—so it claimed—could not locate the missing squad.

Was there a mystery here? Not really. Since the Senators were winning, a too-wet field meant a called game—and a victory for them.

After a half hour, the rain stopped but the field was unplayable, so Washington was declared the winner. However, the next day the Red Sox filed a protest. American League President William Harridge studied the matter for nearly two weeks. On August 28, he declared that it was Washington's responsibility to have a grounds crew available. He ordered the game forfeited to Boston.

Cheapskates

The Stingiest Misers in the Majors

The tightest of the tightwads in baseball are those with the deepest pockets, those owners who make Scrooge look like Santa Claus with a blank check. They've grown rich in baseball while expecting their players to get by on slave wages. Some skinflint owners would rather count nickels in the league cellar than loosen the purse strings to pay for a winning team. For "The Stingiest Misers in the Majors," The Baseball Hall of SHAME inducts the following:

Charles Comiskey
OWNER · CHICAGO WHITE SOX · 1901–36

Charles Comiskey was the Grand Champion of Cheap. His tight fist on the till was a major influence that led to the infamous Black Sox scandal in 1919. Although the players were in on the fix for the money, they also turned to the gamblers out of spite over Comiskey's stinginess and his treatment of them as chattel.

Comiskey was so tight he would make his team play in dirty uniforms just to save a few pennies on the laundry. There were times when he even charged them for having their uniforms washed. When the standard meal allowance around the league was $4 per day on the road, his players had to get by on $3.

But he saved his most outrageous pettiness when it came to paying salaries. While some of the Sox stars were getting $4,000 to $6,000 a year, everyone else in the majors was making much more. Even semipros at the

time could make five grand a year. But not on Comiskey's professional team.

When a player rebelled and asked for a raise, Comiskey callously told him to take it or leave it. And the player had no choice except to remain in bondage to Ol' Massa Charley. Thanks to a tough reserve clause he helped engineer (after his own playing days were over, naturally), the players could have been blackballed from baseball if they tried to jump the White Sox. And some were!

The Sox won the Series in 1917, but a poor showing the next year gave Comiskey the excuse he needed to cut salaries. Poor attendance, less pay, he told the players. But when the Sox were winning big in 1919 and attendance was back up, he still refused to raise salaries.

No one suffered more from the owner's greediness than pitcher Eddie Cicotte. A consistent 20-game winner, Cicotte could never get more out of Comiskey than $3,500 a year. Cicotte won 28 in leading the Sox to the pennant in 1917 and in 1919 was on his way to doing it again. He was motivated by a new clause in his contract that guaranteed him a $5,000 bonus if he won 30 or more games. Eddie notched his 29th victory with three weeks still left in the season and it looked like he'd finally collect that hard-earned bonus. But he never got it. Comiskey benched him with the lame excuse he was saving him for the Series. Cicotte hated Comiskey for cheating him. That bitterness, plus Comiskey's shabby treatment of his other players, had a lot to do with several Sox playing ball with the gamblers in the Series fix.

But that didn't change Comiskey. He showed the world his flinty skin again a few years later with his scandalous treatment of Dickie Kerr. After winning 21 games in 1920 and 19 the following year, Kerr said he wanted more than the $3,500 Comiskey was paying him. Comiskey wouldn't even consider it, so to make a decent living, Kerr accepted $5,000 to play semipro ball. For that affront, Kerr was suspended from baseball.

The New York Yankees
1978

Leave it to the Yankees to come up with an organized campaign in team greediness. Those Penny Pinchers in Pinstripes won the World Series and then voted to give manager Bob Lemon a measly half-share of the purse.

All Lemon had done was come to the rescue of the Yankees on July 25, 1978, and take them from the depths of the second division, 10½ games back, to the world championship. Everyone in baseball attributed the victory to Bob's calm leadership after the stormy reign of Billy Martin.

Everyone, that is, except the Yankee players who gladly lined their own pockets while shortchanging Lemon. In December, after months of bad press detailing their stinginess, the team grudgingly voted to give Lemon a full share after all ($31,236) and held out a half-share for Martin ($15,618).

Cal Griffith
OWNER · WASHINGTON-MINNESOTA, A.L. · 1955–84

Cal Griffith may be out of baseball but the memory of his parsimony lives on.

With Simon Legree as a role model, Griffith was still fighting in the 1980s to continue paying his players in 1970 dollars. In any other business, he might have been charged with violating the federal minimum wage laws.

Griffith's Twins were top-heavy with rookies and unknowns. "We're building from the ground up," was his standard line. But there was method to his miserliness. Rookies, after all, could be paid the major league minimum of $33,500. Included on the 1982 roster, for example, were thirteen rookies and a veteran whose seven years in the bigs made him the club's most experienced player. With a lineup like that, Griffith could hold the average salary down to $65,000 while other teams in the league averaged $190,000.

Griffith didn't like his stingy reputation. "People who call me cheap never had to make a payroll," he said. "I'll pay them (the players) what they deserve and not what their agents think they deserve." Instead of paying what they merited, Griffith traded away or lost to free agency enough talent to field a pennant contender—Bert Blyleven, Lyman Bostock, Bill Campbell, Dan Ford, Larry Hisle, Jerry Koosman, Ken Landreaux, Roy Smalley, Butch Wynegar, Geoff Zahn, and, of course, Rod Carew.

Ed Barrow

PRESIDENT · NEW YORK, A.L. · 1939–45

In his rookie year of 1941, Phil Rizzuto got a bitter introduction to the cheap side of Yankee president Ed Barrow.

Rizzuto hit his first and most memorable home run the second week of the season against the Red Sox in Yankee Stadium. It won the game in the last of the tenth—the classic setup every young player dreams about. A bunch of happy fans came out of the stands to celebrate. As Rizzuto rounded third base, one of the fans grabbed his hat and took off.

The next morning, expecting praise for his heroics, Rizzuto was summoned to Ed Barrow's office. The rookie's jaw fell to the carpet when he heard Barrow's order: Pay for the cap!

It may have been the only time a player was billed by his own team for winning a game.

Harry Frazee

OWNER · BOSTON, A.L. · 1917–23

Harry Frazee cared more for Broadway than he did for baseball and he shamefully sucked his team dry to pay for his show biz lifestyle.

By the time he finished peddling off his high-priced talent to pay his bills, Frazee had turned the Red Sox into the Dead Sox. His real passion was backing Broadway plays that consistently flopped. And he selfishly used his Boston team as a bankroll.

Frazee started unraveling the Red Sox on Jan. 9, 1920, when he sold Babe Ruth to the Yankees for $125,000 and a guaranteed $350,000 mortgage on Fenway Park. The fans were outraged. In 1919, Ruth had set a new major league mark with 29 home runs, but Frazee brushed off criticism of the sale. "Ruth's twenty-nine home runs were more spectacular than useful," he said. "They didn't help the Red Sox get out of sixth place."

Even being hung in effigy after the Ruth sale didn't faze Frazee. He continued to hold down salaries and sell to the Yankees whenever he needed ready cash.

His personal scrimping also was something to behold. In 1919, the club held a Babe Ruth Day to honor the slugger. More than 15,000 fans came out to salute their hero. And Frazee, with amazing generosity, gave the Babe a lousy cigar as a gift. Even worse, Ruth had to buy a ticket for his wife to get her into the Appreciation Day game.

"That Frazee," the Babe growled, "was a cheap son of a bitch!"

Arthur Soden

PRESIDENT · BOSTON, N.L. · 1877–1906

Hugh Duffy was one of the great hitters in the game. In 1894 he set the all-time batting mark with an astonishing .438 average. The year before he had hit .363. With stats like that, Duffy felt justified in asking the Braves front office for a raise.

Incredibly, he was turned down cold. Duffy kept going back with the same request, but team president Arthur Soden refused. They were still arguing when the 1895 season started. Despite the insult, Duffy played and again hit a healthy .352.

Finally, Soden backed down, sort of. He gave Duffy a raise—a magnificent increase of $12.50 a month. He also made Duffy the team captain. But there was nothing honorable about the position. According to his contract, the captain was held responsible for team equipment. Anything missing at the end of the season came out of his pocket. It ended up costing poor Duffy more than he made from the raise.

Turnstile Turnoffs

The Most Undignified Ballpark Promotions

Baseball promotions are a means of scoring big at the gate even if the home team is losing big on the field. Management sometimes has felt that the fans want more than runs, hits, and errors; that the game itself can't make it without some gimmick or giveaways. But some promotions have the taste and sophistication of a TV game show gone mad. For "The Most Undignified Ballpark Promotions," The Baseball Hall of SHAME inducts the following:

Beer Night

MUNICIPAL STADIUM, CLEVELAND · JUNE 4, 1974

The Cleveland Indians management couldn't have been dumber if they had offered free gasoline and matches and invited all the pyromaniacs in town out to the game.

In one of the most boneheaded promotional schemes ever conceived, the Indians offered the fans all the beer they could guzzle at 10 cents a cup. The promotion was nothing more than an open invitation for every thug in town to come to a drunken riot. And that's exactly what the Indians got.

Early in the game against the Texas Rangers, fans started running out on the field and harassing players. As the night wore on and the beer flowed, things turned ugly. Fans started bombarding the Ranger bullpen and dugout with firecrackers and beer.

In the bottom of the ninth inning, with the score tied 5–5, all hell broke loose. The fans, crocked from downing more than 60,000 ten-ounce cups of beer, poured onto the field looking for a fight.

Several menacing fans surrounded Ranger right fielder Jeff Burroughs and then snatched his hat and tried to rip the glove off his hand. When he defended himself, Burroughs was pushed and punched. That's when Ranger manager Billy Martin led his bat-wielding players on a rescue mission to aid their stricken teammate. Even the Indians rushed out to assist the Rangers.

Still, the players were outnumbered by the chair-hurling, bottle-throwing mob. Security guards and hastily summoned city police forcibly quieted the brawlers as the players and umpires made it safely off the field.

Umpire Nestor Chylak, whose hand was cut by a flying chair, ordered the game forfeited to Texas. "The fans were uncontrollable beasts," he fumed. Nine people were arrested and seven were treated at nearby hospitals for minor injuries.

Incredibly, the Cleveland management had scheduled three more 10-cent-beer nights for the season—and still planned to go ahead with them. But American League President Lee MacPhail closed down the Cleveland bar as a health hazard to baseball.

Atlanta Braves Promotions

FULTON COUNTY STADIUM · 1972–79

During the 1970s, the Atlanta Braves spent most of their time down at the bottom of the barrel looking up at the rest of the division. And while they were down there, they scraped together some of the most absurd promotions ever concocted.

The guy who came up with the ludicrous stunts was the Braves publicity director Bob Hope. "Shame is the only word to describe what we did," said Hope. "The Braves finished in last place four straight years. So as long as the team was losing games, we in the promotion department had nothing to lose."

Hope arranged for otherwise sane, normal people to race around on camels and ostriches and throw cow chips at each other. For "Headlock and Wedlock Night," 34 couples were married at home plate in a mass wedding which was followed by professional wrestlers demonstrating their own peculiar embraces.

One bizarre promotion nearly caused a fatality. An Atlanta disc jockey dove head-first into the world's largest ice cream sundae. Nobody told him that ice cream has a consistency like quicksand. The poor guy slowly sank out of sight in the goo. He was almost gone when guards pulled him out and revived him.

Then there was "Wet T-shirt Night" in 1977. "A month into the season we knew we had another last place team," said Hope. "Our attitude was you can't disgrace a disgrace. Anyway, we had long since gone beyond any resemblance of good taste."

The promotion was scheduled to follow the Cubs-Braves game. Although there was a 2½ hour rain delay, the 27,000 fans refused to budge. It's doubtful they stayed because of team loyalty.

During the sixth inning, an announcement was made that registration for the wet T-shirt contest would begin in the picnic area behind the right field foul line. For the rest of the game, as 43 contestants walked one at a time to the registration table, the appreciative crowd accorded each girl the ultimate honor—a standing ovation.

The girls brought more cheers than the Braves who were trounced, 11–0. The game was finally over at 1:30 in the morning and then the action the crowd had been waiting for began. The 43 contestants were drenched by the scores of Atlanta celebrities who had fought like banshees to be judges.

The winner was the daughter of a Methodist minister—a very angry Methodist minister.

Disco Demolition Night

COMISKEY PARK, CHICAGO · JULY 12, 1979

Even White Sox owner Bill Veeck admitted this was a rotten promotion—and he helped dream it up.

Veeck schemed with Chicago disc jockey Steve Dahl of WLUP Radio to give rock fans a chance to demonstrate against the intrusion of disco on the music scene. Veeck and Dahl planned to build a bonfire in center field at Comiskey Park and destroy thousands of disco records brought in by fans who paid a special admission price of 98 cents.

As expected, the stunt backfired and thousands of unruly fans nearly destroyed the field rather than the records.

More than 50,000 disco-hating fans showed up for a double-header against the Detroit Tigers. It took only a few innings before the fans noticed the striking resemblance between a record and a Frisbee. Flying records sailed through the air and the game had to be halted several times to clear the discs off the field. Then other debris pelted the playing area. Players had to dodge firecrackers and Tiger outfielder Ron LeFlore was almost beaned by a golf ball thrown from the stands.

By the time the between-games ceremony began, the fans were primed for action. When a bosomy blonde "fire goddess" named Loreli ignited the bonfire of disco records, it looked like a signal to attack. About 7,000 spectators surged out of the stands and ran wild over the field.

Pleas by Veeck and broadcaster Harry Caray on the public address system fell on deaf ears. A detachment of helmeted police finally cleared the field and arrested more than 50 boisterous youths. At least six people suffered minor injuries.

Umpire Dave Phillips decided that it would be impossible to start the second game because the field had been torn up so badly. The next day, American League President Lee MacPhail forfeited the game to Detroit.

"I'm shocked, amazed and chagrined," Veeck said of the forfeit.

That's exactly how most people felt about the promotion.

Ladies Day

NATIONAL PARK, WASHINGTON, D.C. · 1897

It was a promotion ahead of its time. In 1897, the Washington Senators (then in the National League) introduced the first formal Ladies Day to the nation's capital. To broaden the appeal of the game and to boost the box office take, the ball club invited women to attend free to learn more about the sport. The ladies, it turned out, knew a whole lot more and acted a whole lot differently than management thought.

A mob of pushing, shouting, anything-but-ladylike guests filled the stands at National Park. They focused most of their attention on Senators pitcher George "Winnie" Mercer, the city's heartthrob. Winnie was dazzling on the mound to the delight of his adoring audience.

But Winnie also happened to hate umpires as much as he loved the ladies—and the combination of the two in the same ball park at the same time spelled trouble. The more he baited the umpire, the more the women squealed with glee. But after one heated rhubarb in the fifth inning, umpire Bill Carpenter thumbed Winnie out of the game. The ladies went wild.

Their indignant uproar lasted until the final out when an army of infuriated females poured out of the stands. They surrounded Carpenter, battered him to the ground and ripped his clothing. With the help of some of the players, he fought his way through the mob to the safety of the clubhouse. But the turmoil didn't subside. Angered by his escape, the ladies attacked the stadium. Seats were ripped out, windows and doors were broken, and railings were torn from their moorings before police quelled the disturbance. The umpire had to be smuggled out of the park in disguise. No one dared hold another Ladies Day in Washington for years.

Woeful Windups

The Most Disastrous Farewell Performances

Careers, franchises, stadiums, and seasons must all come to an end sooner or later. Some bow out gracefully. Others exit without a shred of dignity, leaving behind a residue of shame that even the garbageman won't touch. For "The Most Disastrous Farewell Performances," The Baseball Hall of SHAME inducts the following:

Washington Senators' Final Game

SEPT. 30, 1971

The Washington Senators were just one out away from winning their final game in the nation's capital. The franchise was packing up and moving to Texas.

There was a collective lump in the throats of the Senators. With a 7–5 lead, they were all set to give their loyal fans a victory, a going-away gift to remember. Instead, the fans gave the Senators something to remember—a forfeit.

The team was playing its farewell home game against the Yankees at Robert F. Kennedy Memorial Stadium and the 14,460 fans came not so much to cheer the Senators as to express their contempt for owner Bob Short.

Chants of "We Want Short!" throughout the game kept the crowd in a frenzy. The Senators added fuel to the fire with a stirring comeback to take a 7–5 lead in the eighth inning.

Suddenly, a few exuberant fans climbed out of their first base seats and ran around the field trying to shake hands with the players. While they were being shooed away, another 50 more came from the left field bleachers. Play was held up for several minutes until the field was cleared.

Despite the turmoil, the ninth inning got started. Washington pitcher Joe Grzenda got the first two Yankees out. The victory was almost nailed down. But the fans weren't ready to sit by and watch baseball desert them. As Grzenda prepared to pitch to Yankee Horace Clarke, thousands of boisterous fans suddenly erupted in a spontaneous demonstration. Police were powerless as the crowd swarmed over the field. The bases and home plate disappeared instantly. The turf was ripped up. The bullpen roofs nearly collapsed under the weight of dancing fans. Others attacked the scoreboard. The letters, even the lightbulbs, were pulled down for souvenirs.

Within minutes, the game, the ballpark, and the Senators' franchise were in shambles. The game was forfeited to the Yankees. Instead of a final 7–5 triumph, the Senators lost 9–0 and carried that disgrace with them to Texas.

Joe Pignatano

CATCHER · NEW YORK, N.L. · SEPT. 30, 1962

On a dreary, damp day in Chicago during a dull game between the Mets and the Cubs, Joe Pignatano ended his unspectacular six-year career in a most spectacular way. In his very last appearance at the plate as a major leaguer, Pignatano hit into a triple play.

Already losing 5–1, the Mets made a feeble grasp at a comeback with Sammy Drake on second and Richie Ashburn on first and nobody out in the eighth inning. Pignatano, appearing in only his twenty-seventh game of the year, swung late on a fast ball and looped what looked to the runners like a broken-bat single to the right of second base. Drake and Ashburn were off and running. But Cubs second baseman Ken Hubbs caught the ball easily for one out. He flipped the ball to first baseman Ernie Banks to double off Ashburn and Banks fired to second to nab Drake for the third out. A triple play! What an inglorious ending to a career.

The 1904 Season

A season that should have had a bang-up finale instead went whimpering quietly off into winter. The fans were cheated out of a World Series because of the egos of the National League owners and managers and the contempt they had for the upstart American League.

There was no World Series in 1904.

The National League, still smarting from the humiliating loss to the new American League in the first Series the previous year, refused to play. The snub tarnished the entire season and left fans on both sides with a bad taste for "professional" baseball.

Established in 1876, the National League had been considered the majors of baseball for decades. When the American League was organized in 1901, the club owners in the senior circuit were scornful of the new league's playing ability. More important, they resented the competition for the fans and their money the new league represented. But by 1903, the American League was already established with people like Cy Young winning 28 games for the champion Boston Pilgrims (later renamed Red Sox). The powerful National League winners, the Pittsburgh Pirates, condescended to meet the Pilgrims in a best of nine series to determine the "world's championship." To the Pirates' dismay, the Pilgrims whipped them five games to three.

At the end of the 1904 season, the Pilgrims again finished first in their league. The New York Giants, under John McGraw, won the National League title. Once more the World Series challenge was made, but this time Giants President, John T. Brush, sniffed his nose at the idea. The prestige of his team would not be sullied in any contest with minor leaguers, he declared. McGraw agreed, but his reasons were more personal. Before joining the Giants he had feuded with American League President Ban Johnson and this was his way of getting even.

The press and the public screamed in indignation over Brush's refusal to play. But Brush held firm. Publicly, he said the level of play was inferior. Privately, he just didn't want to give any more credibility to the growing American League competition in New York.

Without a Series to settle the matter, the Pilgrims proclaimed themselves world champions by default. The Giants were declared Shirkers of the Year—also by default.

Connie Mack Stadium's Final Game

PHILADELPHIA · OCT. 1, 1970

After six decades of faithful service (43 years known as Shibe Park) Connie Mack Stadium deserved a decent, dignified farewell. It didn't get one. Seconds after the final out of the final game, the fans turned the stadium into a staging area for raiding pirates, besmirching all that the park had stood for.

The Phillies management wanted to go out in grand style. They had dozens of prizes, including a new automobile, to give to fans in ceremonies following the game against the Expos. But they also worried about rowdiness and brought in 200 extra police. What they really needed was the 82nd Airborne.

To forestall souvenir hunting, the Phillies distributed a seat slat to each fan as a remembrance. Their intentions may have been good, but the results were disastrous. In the hands of the unruly crowd, the slats quickly became weapons. They were used as clubs and hurled like spears. No one in the stands was safe from assault and even the players took the field at their own risk. At one point, a bunch of the bozos came out of the stands onto the outfield. One of them grabbed Phillies left fielder Ron Stone as he circled under a fly ball. Stone missed the catch allowing Montreal to score the tying run.

In the bottom of the tenth, the Phils' Oscar Gamble drove in Tim McCarver with the winning run and the mob went wild. Using everything from their bare hands to the hatchet-like slats, roving bands of marauders ripped apart the old stadium. They didn't steal the kitchen sink, but one of the crazies did dismantle a toilet and staggered home with it. By the time the mob had completed its destruction, the park was in shambles and the farewell ceremonies were cancelled.

Who Else Belongs in The Baseball Hall of SHAME?

Do you have any nominations for The Baseball Hall of SHAME? Give us your picks as we select more shameful, embarrassing, deplorable, blundering, and boneheaded moments in baseball history for the Hall's second induction ceremonies. Here's your opportunity to pay a light-hearted tribute to the game we all love.

On separate sheets of paper, describe your nominations in detail. Those nominations which are documented with the greatest amount of facts such as anecdotes, first-hand accounts, newspaper or magazine clippings, box scores or photos, have the best chance of being inducted into The Baseball Hall of SHAME. Feel free to send as many nominations as you wish.

If you don't find a new or existing category that fits your nomination, then make up your own category. If your nomination is selected, you will be sent a certificate officially recognizing you as a member of The Baseball Hall of SHAME Selection Committee.

Mail your nominations to: The Baseball Hall of SHAME, P.O. Box 6218, West Palm Beach, FL 33405. All submitted material becomes the property of The Baseball Hall of SHAME and is nonreturnable.

In addition to those categories already included in the book, the Hall has listed 20 new categories in need of nominations. They are:

- GO AWAY, KID, YA BOTHER ME!
  The Rudest Players to Get Autographs From
- A STAR-DUDDED AFFAIR
  The Most Disgraceful Episodes in All-Star Game History
- ANYTHING FOR A BUCK
  The Most Tasteless Commercial Endorsements by Players and Managers
- GET THE LEAD OUT!
  Players Whose Lack of Hustle Cost Their Teams Critical Games
- LOCKER ROOM LOCKOUT
  Players Most Hostile to the Media
- POPCORN, PEANUTS AND . . . BELLYACHES!
  The Most Wretched Concession Food and Drink at Ballparks
- PARTING SHOTS
  The Most Unsportsmanlike Reactions of Players Taken Out of Games
- BULL *!?/# PENS
  The Cheapest Shots Taken by Sportswriters at Players and Teams
- STUFFING THE BALLOT BOX
  The Most Unconscionable Voting for Baseball Awards
- BOGUS BABIES
  High-Priced Rookies Who Failed Miserably in the Big Leagues
- BROADCAST BONERS
  The Worst Gaffes and Bloopers by Announcers
- COSTLY CUTUPS
  Players' Stupid Antics That Turned Out to be Costly Injuries
- LAST LICKS
  The Snidest Remarks Made by a Player About his Former Team
- A KICK IN THE TEETH
  The Most Despicable Treatment of Players by Team Management
- DOWN ON THE FAT FARM
  The Most Out-of-Shape Players and Teams
- BLOOPERSTOWN
  The Most Flagrant Omissions from Baseball's Hall of Fame

- THREE JEERS FOR THE WINNERS!
  Baseball's Most Ungracious Winners
- DOLLAR SIGNS OF THE TIMES
  The Greediest Players and Agents Who Ever Negotiated a Contract
- SCOUTING RETORTS
  The Most Boneheaded Scouting Reports—"Can't Miss" Prospects
  Who Bombed Out and "Can't Make" Prospects Who Became Su-
  perstars
- HEAVE HO-HO'S
  The Most Inglorious Ejections from a Game

Photo by Lynn T Spence—*St. Louis Post Dispatch*

The Winning Team

The establishment of The Baseball Hall of SHAME is the realization of a lifelong dream for its two founders:

Bruce Nash has felt the sting of baseball shame ever since he smashed a sure triple in a Pee Wee League game and was almost thrown out at first base because he was so slow afoot. He graduated to Little League but "played" his first and only season without ever swinging at a pitch. His most embarrassing moment on the field occurred in a sandlot game when a misjudged fly ball bounced off his head allowing the winning run to score. As a die-hard Dodger fan in Brooklyn, Nash was so traumatized by the team's surprise departure that he ended up rooting for the Yankees.

Allan Zullo is an expert on losers. He rooted for the Chicago Cubs during their long cellar-dwelling years. Playing baseball throughout his childhood, he patterned himself after his Cub heroes. That explains why his longest hit in the Pony League was a pop fly double that the first baseman lost in the sun. As a park league coach, Zullo achieved the distinction of piloting a team that did not hit a fair ball in either game of a double–header. Unaccustomed to the Cubs' extraordinary success in 1984, Zullo has switched allegiances—to the Cleveland Indians.

Compiling and maintaining records is the important task of the Hall's curator, **Bernie Ward**. His baseball days during his childhood followed a consistent and predictable pattern—consistently awful and predictably short. His teammates called him "the executioner" because he killed so many of his team's rallies by striking out or hitting into inning-ending double plays.